# Real Estate Wealth Diversification

Simon Tim Muwanguzi

Copyright © 2017 *by Simon Tim Muwanguzi*

Published by Powerhouse Publications

All rights reserved. The author asserts their moral right under the Copyright, Designs and Patents Act 1988 to be identified as the author of this work.

Except for the quotation of small passages for the purposes of criticism and review, no part of this publication may be reproduced, stored in a retrieval system, or transmitted, in any form or by any means, electronic, mechanical, photocopying, recording or otherwise, except under the terms of the Copyright, Designs and Patents Act 1988 without the prior consent of the publisher.

This book is dedicated to
Olivia "Sond" Muwanguzi

www.timoseks.com

## Contents

Foreword ............................................................... 7

Introduction ........................................................... 9

Chapter 1: Why Choose Property?
*The investment realm for all*............................................ 15

Chapter 2: The UK Appeal
*Why we love it so*...................................................... 22

Chapter 3: Entering the Arena
*An overview of investment types, target market and the auction process*................................................. 28

Chapter 4: The Importance of Location & Timing
*Featuring the UK's property hotspots* ........................... 45

Chapter 5: Financing & Mortgages
*Options for financing and repayment*........................... 58

Chapter 6: Residential Investment
*Property type options* .................................................. 82

Chapter 7: Commercial Investment
*Choices and use classes* ............................................... 94

Chapter 8: Land & Other Development Options
*Plot potential, how to develop, asset stripping and more* .................................................................. 107

Chapter 9: Wealth Diversification Tactics
*Spreading risk for maximum returns* ............................ 125

Chapter 10: Building Your Portfolio
*Assessing risk and strategy, plus flip tips and how to break barriers* ...................................................... 134

Chapter 11: Property Law & Conveyancing
*Tax basics and conveyancing stages* ............................. 155

Chapter 12: Further Considerations
*Independent advice, company registration, property investment syndicates* .................................. 164

Chapter 13: My Personal Journey
*Pursuing the dream* ....................................................... 178

Chapter 14: Additional Resources
*The Planning Permission Process* .................................. 185
*Tips to Improve Your Credit Rating* ............................... 188
*Top 10 UK Auction Houses for Property* ....................... 193
*Buy-to-Let / Need-to-Know* ............................................ 196
*Glossary of Property Terms* ........................................... 199
*Useful Contacts* ............................................................. 208

Chapter 15: Timo Real Estate Solutions
*The One-Stop Shop* ....................................................... 213

Acknowledgements ................................................... 222

## Foreword

Having read Simon Tim Muwanguzi's first book, *Property Investment: Create Your Own Legacy*, I was thrilled to learn he was keen to add to his publishing repertoire!

With a seemingly endless amount of investment strategy information available to the masses these days, industry jargon is often hard to digest for the average aspiring property investor. Not so with Simon! His latest book is another gem offering clear and uncomplicated guidance specifically aimed at advising aspiring investors, particularly those who are based overseas, on how to break into property investment in the United Kingdom.

Through explaining the strategies of wealth development techniques, the fundamentals of property investment and portfolio building, Simon covers all considerations, including how to overcome your own personal obstacles, to guide you into making the most of the lucrative strategy that is Real Estate Wealth Diversification.

In his easy-to-understand and warm manner, Simon demonstrates how any one of us can take advantage of the enormous opportunities that the UK property market holds.

Enjoy!

*Nichola Tyrrell,*
Editor.

## Introduction

Having recently published my first book, *Property Investment: Create Your Own Legacy*, which teaches the basics of achieving wealth through property investment, I realised I want to share with my fellow overseas investors how the United Kingdom holds enormous opportunity for them too. Furthermore, I am keen to share the principles of wealth diversification for real estate, which will enable you to reduce your risk while at the same time maximising your investment returns.

As an immigrant from Uganda who has lived in London for more than 20 years, working as a Property and Mortgage consultant for over ten years, I have amassed a vast amount of experience and knowledge of the UK real estate industry. I have assisted many local clients and also several who are based overseas, mainly in the Middle East, Asia and Africa, to invest in and develop a range of UK properties. The lure of the United Kingdom to those from the Middle East, Asia or Africa is longstanding and justified, owing to the nation's stable economy but also its colourful history, affluent and prosperous society, its art and culture. Who wouldn't want to be a part of it?! With the development of communication technology, the world is seemingly smaller. No longer is the UK a world away from the Middle East, Asia or Africa, nor is it necessarily a once-in-a-lifetime dream holiday destination – your location does not restrict your potential to partake in UK investment opportunities!

The dynamics of the real estate industry are more or less the same worldwide; the ideas and suggestions contained within this book are relevant not only to your UK projects, but also in your home country. By sharing my knowledge and offering my services, I hope to not only give you the tools to embark upon your UK investment dreams, but also to encourage and motivate you on your journey of making serious money from UK property investment.

What makes property investment so appealing and fascinating to me, personally, is that one can make an enormous amount of money from just enjoying one's home over an extended period of time. If you own your property long term, you will accumulate a lot of equity in it. If you own a home in a hotspot such as London, it is entirely possible to double your investment within a decade or so. Where else can you earn such high profit without doing anything at all? Imagine what can be accomplished if you don't sit on the property but choose to use the equity to buy other property or indeed renovate, extend and improve it for even further value! Professional property developers refurbishing mid-level homes, for example, commonly earn a very comfortable living from only one or two 'buy-to-sell-quickly' projects per year.

For many people, the idea of property investment sounds enticing in theory but, in reality, many potential investors get cold feet. Worries concerning finance, lack of knowledge, experience, qualifications, may be stopping you from taking that first step. Perhaps you already own a property and dream of creating a vast portfolio but you are not a natural risk-taker. Rest assured, I intend to ease any anxiety and build your confidence and, most importantly, give you the necessary knowledge to make informed decisions regarding your property investment future. I want to share with you my solutions to the barriers that are preventing you from moving forward in property investment, whether it be a poor credit rating, lack of experience or just plain lack of funds to start with! As an investor who has found success, lost almost everything, then rebuilt my investment business from the ground up a second time, I fully understand, on a personal level, the apprehension that may be holding you back. The fact that you have purchased this book is a clear indicator that you are indeed ready to take that first step!

Before delving into the first chapter, take a moment to review why you are drawn to property as an investment. Are you looking for general investment opportunities for the goal of financial freedom and early retirement? Are you looking for a fairly short-term scheme to raise funds for your children's education or to help look after your parents? Are you enticed by the prestige of becoming a property tycoon, owning multiple homes and commercial premises, developing and renting out several properties? Would you just like a UK holiday home for your family and friends to enjoy, renting out in between vacations? A legacy to leave to your children? Whatever your goals in life, I sincerely hope my knowledge and advice will help you to achieve them.

To facilitate your journey on the road to UK property success, my company — Timo Real Estate Solutions — offers a tailor-made comprehensive package and

## Introduction

bespoke personal service at our one-stop-shop for the overseas investor. Our commitment to you:

- We, in partnership with our experienced Business Associates, will make the necessary travel arrangements, including flights and accommodation, for you to travel to the UK to view and buy your property.
- Once you are here, our priority is to find the right residential or commercial property for you at reduced or discounted prices.
- We, in conjunction with the necessary lender or brokerage firm, will also arrange the most suitable mortgage or commercial finance for you, based on your own circumstances and preferences.
- We will also ensure that your new property is managed well so that you can start making money on your investment from day one!
- As part of our excellent After-Sales Service, we also offer other services (sometimes through our reliable intermediaries) like safe and quick money transfers, insurance to cover and protect your investment, as well as property sales if and when you wish to sell your

property investments in a few years' time to make the most of the capital growth.

\* \* \* \* \* \* \* \* \*

Applicable to every potential investor, regardless of location and level of experience, this book explains in detail the exciting world of property investment in the UK, from how to find discounted properties, selecting those with development potential in the right locations, to obtaining financing when your options seem limited; how to choose wisely for a 'quick flip' or a long-term rental investment; how to plan your portfolio strategically and overcome barriers that prevent you from taking the first step – all this and more you will find in the following chapters. Growing a property portfolio of 3, 5, 10 or more investments may seem incredibly ambitious, but it is entirely possible with reliable advisors and management of your portfolio through wealth diversification techniques.

Let's get started with discussing why property in general is such a rewarding means of investment.

# Chapter 1
# Why Choose Property?

## *The investment realm for all*

Why invest in property? The answer is simple – no other investment realm offers as great a potential for profit and security with virtually guaranteed appreciation over time.

We all enjoy our homes. But it is more than a haven in which to relax and build memories with one's family. It is literally a bricks-and-mortar ticket that can lead to financial freedom, if you so desire. Take, for example, an apartment I purchased in East London several years ago. In 2001, I paid £85,000 for it; did some minor decorating and refurbishment and enjoyed living there. Six years later, I sold the flat for £145,000. As this was my main home I was not in a hurry to decorate, I took my time. I had bought it as a home, not a business venture. However, had I bought this flat with pure investment in mind, I could have completed the refurbishments and sold the flat for a good profit much sooner, obtaining a nice tidy sum for further investment elsewhere.

## THE DEMAND

We all need a place to sleep at night, a place to call home, whether it be an apartment, cottage, townhouse or mansion. We may buy a home. We may rent a home. For this reason, there will always be a demand for properties; there will always be opportunities for the property investor. In towns and cities especially, to which people from around the world gravitate in search of employment and better opportunities, the demand for residences will always exist. Regardless of personal wealth, the fortunate rich will always need a home and so too the 'not so rich'. In an economic downturn, people may not be looking to purchase a new property, but there will always be those who require rental properties. There are potential investments everywhere; notice any 'for sale' signs on your next journey to work or the school run. Can you see any potential? An end-of-terrace house that is crying out for an extension? A ramshackle house that, with some decoration and landscaping, could be a real beauty? Or perhaps it could be transformed into a block of flats for long-term rental income or individual re-sale? No matter what level you are at on the property ladder, there is bound to be an opportunity in your area that you just haven't discovered yet.

## THE SECURITY

Putting your hard-earned money into property has long been considered one of the safest and most reliable avenues of investment, particularly when you compare it to stocks and shares, retail and other business ventures. Whether your property is in London, Hong Kong, Dubai, Nairobi or New York, it will never lose value in the long term. Depending on national and international economics, it may appreciate slowly or quickly, or perhaps not at all for a short while. It is certain, though, that eventually it **will** increase in value over time. The rental market is also a safe bet for those interested in earning a long-term, steady income from a property as it gradually gains equity over time.

Rest assured, property prices usually keep pace with the cost of living increases and as such could be a perfect hedge against inflation. It is for this reason that many people in the UK these days are choosing to invest in property rather than pension funds or other assets, such as stocks and shares, that do not offer the same security.

## ANYONE CAN DO IT

Another attractive feature of property investment is that you can start at any level. Formal qualifications are not required. Equipment (other than a telephone and computer) is not required. You can start with smaller properties requiring minimal renovation and progress to more extensive 'heavy development' projects (if you so wish), gaining experience and knowledge along the way. It is more straightforward if you have a sum of money saved up to start with, to use as a deposit for your first investment property, with a percentage put aside for various conveyancing fees, renovation costs, etc. Once your first investment property has been renovated and sold (or rented out) on time and within budget, you will have a track record, based on which mortgage lenders are more open to offering higher loans for more complex projects in the future.

## DON'T BE AFRAID OF THE 'M' WORD

Mortgage! It is not a complicated business to obtain a mortgage in the UK. A mortgage is basically just a big loan. In fact, obtaining a £500,000 mortgage for a residential property is far easier than borrowing an unsecured loan of £30,000 from any UK bank. Most lenders prefer lending where property is the physical collateral. If you have a clean credit history and the basic requisites such as proof of identity, address and income, you will likely be approved for a mortgage within the means allowed for by your deposit / down payment figure.

Is there any other safe way to obtain such a large loan that you can use to increase your own wealth? No. Get your mortgage. Renovate your property. Sell it for a good profit margin or rent it out, all in a matter of months. Use the bank's money to make money for yourself.

If you are based overseas, you need not worry. It is still possible to obtain a UK mortgage. Refer to the upcoming *Financing & Mortgages* and *The UK Appeal* chapters to find out all you need to know regarding requirements for foreign investors.

**EQUITY RELEASE**

Do we want to sell up, buy a new property and move the family every time we've renovated our home to obtain our equity? Not really. There is another way to do it – re-mortgage to obtain equity release. It is possible to release the equity in your current property through re-mortgaging (without paying any taxes). This enables you to obtain a sum of your equity for a multitude of purposes, e.g. renovating or extending the property, general family costs or, you guessed it... a deposit for the purchase of another property!

## YOUR TEAM

With initiative, and reliable advisors, your new property is sure to provide a decent capital gain on re-sale or a nice constant income should you choose to rent it out. If you have a good team of people working for you, the whole process can be a smooth and swift business. Your team may include solicitors, accountants, builders, architects, estate agents, letting agents, to name a few. That's a lot of people.

As an overseas investor, consider a 'one-stop shop' to deal with all these team members. A property investment consultancy such as Timo Real Estate Solutions takes away all the stress for the overseas investor. With Timo Real Estate Solutions acting on your behalf, you need not worry about dealing with local issues from a long distance. With a reliable team working for you in the UK, your property business can be a lucrative side-line to a career in your home country. If you have the ambition and vision, your team will help you see it through from conception to completion, and beyond, all within a specified schedule and budget.

## WHY THE UNITED KINGDOM?

From a global perspective, the UK, particularly London and its surrounding counties, is among the world's most sought-after locations for investment. Its standardised real estate market and legal system are appealing for the overseas investor. Imagine the prestige of owning a London apartment, commercial premises, a country estate?! It is a vibrant, multi-cultural region that welcomes overseas investors. Investors are now looking beyond London, too, with southern and midland market towns as well as northern cities boasting increasing investments due to a less competitive marketplace. Turn to the following chapter for an in-depth review of why investors are favouring UK property over other investment assets.

# Chapter 2
# The UK Appeal

*Why we love it so*

Investors and migrants the world over are lured to the United Kingdom and have been for decades. Why do we love it so? What makes it tick? And why in particular is it a great outlet for overseas investors, both in London and, increasingly, other regions?

**POLITICAL AND ECONOMIC CLIMATES**

The UK has one of the best democracies in the world. It is a nation of peace compared to instability and unrest in many other nations. It is among the world's top five thriving economies, making it relatively stable and prosperous.

**TAXATION LEGISLATION**

Compared with many countries, the UK has highly favourable taxation legislation regarding property purchases. Hong Kong and Singapore, for example, have much higher Stamp Duty rates than the UK, up to 20% in some cases.

## MULTICULTURAL SOCIETY

The United Kingdom, comprising England, Wales, Scotland and Northern Ireland, has a heavily multicultural society with a skilled labour force. It has long been a final resting place of successive waves of immigrants through Europe. The second half of the $20^{th}$ century in particular saw a huge influx from the lands of the former Commonwealth, particularly the West Indies and Pakistan. The early $21^{st}$ century saw Eastern Europeans flock here in droves – nearly half a million since 2000!

## GEOGRAPHY

More or less in the centre of the world, it is handy for Europe (despite Brexit!) and is mid-way between Asia and North America with a temperate climate that suits most people. For a relatively small, island nation, the United Kingdom boasts a remarkable variation of landscapes, from the mountains of Scotland in the north to the flat fenlands of eastern England, the rugged moors of the West Country to the green valleys of Wales.

## HISTORY

Colourful testaments to the UK's rich history are undeniable: remnants of ancient Roman ruins, the mystical Stonehenge, castles and ruins of ancient Anglo-Saxon and Norman invasions, for example. The nation's influence on the rest of the world has been immense, including accomplished historical periods such as the Age of Maritime Exploration, the Industrial Revolution and Victorian Britain, to name a few.

With its incredible history and architecture, arts and culture, beautiful countryside, famous landmarks, the royal family, and London – the best city in the world (in my humble opinion!), the UK's draw to tourists is well justified and stronger than ever. This appeal is not only alluring to tourists, but also migrants and investors. In terms of the property industry, there are some key features that, when combined, make the UK a hotbed of investment opportunity:

1. The education system in the UK is admired the world over. A testament to that is the high percentage of overseas students in the private boarding schools. The majority of overseas students hail from China, India, Nigeria and Malaysia. Many graduates remain in the UK,

contributing their skills and talent to the workforce, which in turn adds to the prosperity and affluence of UK society.
2. Prosperity attracts migrants, and so the population has steadily grown over the decades. Immigration has always been high in the UK, not just for the welfare-state democracy but for job opportunities and great education, as well as free benefits such as the National Health Service.
3. The influx of immigrants over time has led to a chronic housing shortage in the UK. In turn, rent and property sale prices have risen steadily over the long term.
4. The result of all the above has meant the country has, overall, enjoyed a long-stable, prosperous economy. Of course, the UK did suffer during the last recession, as most countries did, but it has recovered nicely in the aftermath.
5. Since Brexit, at the time of writing, the value of the pound has dropped slightly, but the general outlook is positive and this temporary drop makes the UK a buyer's market for foreign investors.

You can see how these features link together — a matter of cause and effect! With all the above in mind, the UK property market is considered a safe yet highly profitable route for property investors.

According to London Estate Agents, Chesterton Humberts, investors from China, Russia, Nigeria and the Middle East have been particularly keen to invest in UK property in recent years, likely due to growing political and economic strife in their own countries.

Let's look at, for example, a landmark building in London that has been targeted for development by foreign investors for many years.

Battersea Power Station, decommissioned from its original use over 30 years ago, has been a hot topic for property developers. The former coal-powered plant, towering over the south bank of the Thames, has always been a landmark (some say an eyesore!). Over the years developers have considered all manner of development proposals, from turning it into a football stadium, a massive hotel, and a children's theme park. All these plans were dropped for one reason or another. Recently, a group of Malaysian developers accepted the challenge, to the tune of a whopping GBP £8 billion investment, to convert the old power station to a 39-acre mixed-use complex of flats, shops and offices.

This is an example of major foreign investment on the grandest of scales; it is, in fact, one of several high-value developments in progress in the United Kingdom. You don't have to be a billionaire to enter the UK property arena, of course. My advice is to start small and steady – the classic story of the tortoise and the hare comes to mind!

\* \* \* \* \* \* \* \* \*

The following chapter covers important options to consider before taking that first step on the property ladder, including which type of development to pursue and how to find a bargain-price property!

# Chapter 3
# Entering the Arena

*An overview of investment types, target market and the auction process*

In its simplest terms, 'property investment' entails the purchase of a residential or commercial premises as a business opportunity to gain income. Whether you buy a property with the intention of refurbishing and selling quickly (commonly known as 'flipping'), undertaking major renovation, or retaining the property as a long-term rental opportunity and awaiting gradual value appreciation, the end purpose is to achieve as much capital growth as possible.

In the United Kingdom, residential properties include apartments, or flats, as well as houses (both detached and semi-detached) of varying sizes. Garden space may be vast or, particularly in London, non-existent! Commercial properties range from isolated out-of-town warehouses and industrial parks to tiny, yet highly sought-after London office and retail units and everything in between. Opportunities for both domestic and overseas investors are virtually limitless.

## TYPES OF INVESTMENT

### The Quick Flip

The key to success in obtaining the quickest sale and return on your investment is selecting the right property from the outset – one that is already attractive to buyers but will become even more sought after once you have refurbished it. Buy it at the lowest price possible, refurbish to a quality, modernised standard, then get it back on the market as soon as possible. Refurbishment may include some quite heavy renovations, from knocking down a wall to create an open-plan kitchen/diner, updating the entire bathroom and replacing windows and the boiler, or perhaps, if you're lucky, it may just need a fresh coat of paint throughout. Don't forget any outside space too – landscape gardening may be required to get your property ready to re-sell. It is imperative, for this type of investment, to have reliable and talented builders who are, above all, speedy. The quicker you refurbish, the quicker you can sell it!

## The Major Renovation

The scope for renovation doesn't end there. Take, for example, a 2-bedroom terraced house. After council planning permission has been sought and approved, you could extend this to include a couple of extra bedrooms with a loft conversion and en-suite bathrooms. With a ground-floor flat, you could also add a conservatory if the outside space allows. In ground-floor city dwellings, where car parking space is severely restricted, adapting a small outdoor space to an authorised parking area would add untold value. While there is considerable cost in renovating to this extent, also adding substantial time to the process while seeking permission from the relevant authorities, the re-sale value increases accordingly with the expanded space and features.

## The Long Game

If your preference is to purchase a property for the long term, renting it out to tenants is your best option to ensure a steady income stream while the property gradually increases in value over time. In this case, the short-term fluctuations of the property market are somewhat irrelevant as you are playing 'the long game' and are more interested in values over the next five, ten or even twenty years when property is sure to appreciate substantially. The bonus here is that your tenants are paying your mortgage, probably more, giving you a guaranteed monthly cash flow (provided the property is constantly occupied). From the point of view of an overseas investor, it is highly recommended you engage the services of a letting agent who can act on your behalf to ensure you have a constant, reliable tenant in place and who can deal with any issues that arise.

## BROADENING YOUR TARGET MARKET

Whichever type of property you choose to invest in, selling to the widest target market is paramount. The more potential buyers to which your property appeals, the quicker you can sell and the greater chance you have of increasing your sales price. You may even get a bidding war on your hands! I will cover the importance of location in detail shortly, but it is worth mentioning here that, with residential properties, the proximity to schools and general amenities is crucial. Your property may be ideal for a young family in your eyes, but if it is nowhere near a school, buyers with children won't even consider it. When you are just starting out in the investment world, it is also a good idea to steer clear of large, expensive 'specialist' properties that have a limited appeal as only high-end buyers can afford them. The same applies in this case with commercial property. It takes time to acquire the knowledge and experience that is needed for taking on the big investment and redevelopment projects. Start small, learn the ropes, then progress to the higher value properties.

## STAYING OBJECTIVE

When you invest in a property – financially and physically – it can be difficult to remain objective and not become emotionally tied to the project. It is important to maintain perspective: this is your **business** venture, not an interior design hobby or your own permanent home. Don't get tangled up in the process of choosing which bedroom doors to replace and picking the right paint colour for the entrance hall. The goal is to make money – for yourself, your family, your future. Do only what is required to complete the refurbishment to the desired standard – within budget and on time – then either sell it or rent it out. Walk away confident and content, knowing you have completed a quality finished project and move on to your next investment.

## PROPERTY OWNERSHIP OPTIONS

In the UK, it is important to remember that there are different categories when it comes to which type of property ownership you may be offered when looking to purchase. Overall there are three types of ownership: freehold, leasehold and the lesser-known commonhold.

*Freehold* means that the owner of the land, or freeholder/landlord, has total ownership of the property or land indefinitely, with complete control over the property subject to planning permission and any mortgage lender restrictions, if applicable. This also means the freeholder bears full and sole responsibility for maintenance and repairs of the property.

*Leasehold* means that a leaseholder has the ownership of the property for a period of time which has been granted by the freeholder. The date at which a lease expires is specified and can range from a few years up to 999 years. When the lease expires, ownership of the property reverts to the freeholder. However, the existing leases on properties are usually no longer than a couple of hundred years these days and mainly apply to flats or apartments. Leaseholders are able to purchase an extension of the lease if desired. As a leaseholder, it is also possible to purchase the freehold if the landlord is interested in selling it.

*Commonhold* is a relatively new type of property ownership available only in England and Wales. It was introduced in 2004 and is applicable to owners of one or more freehold properties (usually flats) within a building that has significant common areas (such as hallways, a foyer, gardens, a carpark, etc.). These common parts of the building contractually form part of what is known as a commonhold development. A Commonhold Association, comprising the individual freeholders, own and manage the common parts. Members meet regularly to discuss and vote on various issues concerning maintenance, repairs and improvements.

**FINDING A BARGAIN**

As an investor, you obviously want to purchase property for the lowest price possible – a bargain! The best way to find a bargain? At an auction house. Auction houses are a popular destination for investors looking to purchase property at below market value.

There are several reasons why a property might be sold at auction.

Properties selling at auction are often repossessions, meaning that the owner, for whatever reason, did not keep up the mortgage payments and the bank/building society has been forced to take back possession of the property. The bank/building society is now keen to sell this property as a matter of urgency at a price that, at the very least, pays off the outstanding mortgage sum. As such the properties sell fast and at a fraction of their current market value; the banks just want to pay off the outstanding mortgage and get back to business as soon as possible.

Not all auction properties, though, are repossessions being sold by mortgage lenders. Private individuals also sell property at auction, for a variety of reasons. The owner may be going through a divorce, have debts to clear, may have suffered a death in the family, or may be planning to move overseas and therefore want a quick sale. It may be that the owner is prepared to drop the price for the convenience of offloading the property as soon as possible, and is willing to forego some potential earnings. In fact, you may even already be acquainted with someone in one of these situations. While it is opportunistic to take advantage of someone else's possible misfortune, the seller involved may welcome the suggestion of a quick private sale rather than go through the auction house process.

Landlords also use the auction house to sell property quickly. In the case of a landlord needing to release equity for investment in a new development, the auction house is the quickest way of doing so. For new property investors, it is recommended you attend a couple of auctions merely as a spectator, to get a feel for the process before going down that route yourself.

## THE PROPERTY AUCTION PROCESS

There are two methods through which you can buy or sell a property through an auction:

- You can employ the services of a local, reputable agent who specialises in sourcing or selling properties for their clients through auction houses.
- You can do it yourself. It may appear a daunting process but rest assured that when you do your research and due diligence well in advance, you shall be pleasantly surprised that

it's not a very complicated exercise after all. In fact, you may enjoy it so much that it turns out to be a new career! Just think about it for a second... how many jobs in the world give you that sense of satisfaction and at the same time you make a lot of money?

## STEPS TO BUYING AND SELLING PROPERTY AT AN AUCTION HOUSE:

Firstly, it's a good idea to attend a few auctions prior to the one in which you intend to bid or sell. This will help you become familiar with how the whole process works and gain confidence going forward. If you wish to sell a property at auction, your best course of action is to use the services of auction house staff to advise and guide you accordingly. If you're looking to bid, follow the steps below for a stress-free auction experience!

1. **Research auction houses** – 'Google' local property and auction websites in your area and order their latest catalogues – these contain information about the next available dates for the auctions, guide prices and any other relevant details. Equally important are the local newspapers which often list details of

upcoming auctions in the area. You'll find a list of the country's top 10 auction houses at the end of this chapter.

2. **Do the maths** – Work out your budget, perhaps with the assistance of your accountant, so that you don't end up outbidding yourself on the day. Auction houses require a good degree of discipline, calm and composure as you strive to get your desired property at the lowest price possible. It's a skill that you shall learn in due course.

3. **Choose an auction property** – It is very important to do your homework before attending an auction to bid as once you raise your paddle, there is no going back! Once you've browsed the auction house catalogues and have found a property that interests you, arrange a viewing through the auctioneers as soon as possible, well BEFORE the auction date. Catalogues are generally published about four weeks prior to auction, so you need to act fast. It may be necessary to view the property in the company of a builder and/or architect and surveyor whose expertise could come in handy in terms of not only working out all the facts and figures regarding any refurbishment,

but also in terms of helping you make an informed decision whether to buy this property at all.

4. **Contact your solicitor** – Once you've found your property and decided it's a good bet for your investment portfolio, contact your conveyancing solicitor (one experienced in auction transactions) to discuss how the whole conveyancing process shall work during the buying process at the auction. You need to ensure your solicitor is available and willing to undertake the conveyancing straightaway. You will also want your solicitor to examine the auctioneer's legal pack regarding the property. It is very important to remember that once the hammer is hit, you have only 28 days to exchange contracts and complete the purchase transaction. Moreover, you must pay a 10% deposit on auction day which in many instances, may not be refundable if you fail to complete the transaction in time. For this reason, a good solicitor on standby can guide you through this speedy and, sometimes, complicated process.

The seller of a property through auction should also seek advice from their solicitors but this is not as stringent as for the buyer.

5. **Have funds available / mortgage offer in place** – If you are buying this property outright, for cash on the day, then the whole process can be very straightforward. If, on the other hand, you need a mortgage to make this purchase, it is imperative that you obtain the mortgage offer from your lender prior to the auction date. Use a reliable mortgage broker or consultant who is already familiar with buying properties through auctions. Rest assured that the right one will effectively take the stress away from you.

6. **On the day, keep calm!** – Having done your research, consulted advisors, prepared your finances, attend the auction armed with all necessary documents, including (and where applicable): proof of identity, valuation report from a surveyor, building estimates, solicitor's report, mortgage offer, cheque or credit card details for payment of the 10% deposit, to mention but a few. Arrive early to get a good seat so the auctioneer can easily spot you. Remember that the guide price is generally set

much lower than what the property is likely to sell for. The seller will have also agreed a confidential reserve price (the minimum acceptable sale price) with the auctioneer. This may be up to 10% higher than the guide price.

7. **Don't despair!** – If your bid doesn't win the property, don't despair – there is always another auction! The only real downside is that you will have lost your preparation costs spent on the survey, solicitor's report and the auction house admin fee (generally around £300).

8. **My bid was accepted!** – You're bid has been accepted... now what?! The excitement of the bidding is over and you can let your hair down and celebrate. But first, as soon as the hammer drops, you will be required to produce your proof of identity (usually two pieces) and your deposit payment of 10% of the sale price. The remaining balance will be due in 28 days. You will be given a legally binding contract that eventually will enable you to purchase the property. Now, off to celebrate...

## REPRESENTATION

Searching for property is a time-consuming task at the best of times, even more so if you are thousands of miles away! Not to mention overseeing renovation, dealing with lettings, and eventually selling your properties. As an overseas investor, the benefits of having a one-stop-shop agent to act on your behalf are immeasurable. Be sure to engage the services of a knowledgeable, experienced and above all, trustworthy local property investment agent.

While you don't need to be resident here to invest in property, it is advisable that you visit the United Kingdom in order to view any properties from which you can choose to buy. It is not compulsory to do so by any means, but given my experience I would strongly encourage you to be directly involved throughout the buying process from day one!

It is also imperative that you or your agent identifies a good solicitors' firm that shall advise you accordingly about any legal matters regarding your purchase, help you to exchange contracts and complete, as well as registering your new property with the UK Land Registry.

Once you have successfully purchased your investment property, there are other matters to consider like finding tenants and management, insuring the building and its contents as well as payment of the bills such as Council Tax, electricity and gas. As you are based abroad, it may be a good idea to hire the services of a good property management agent to do all this on your behalf.

## LET'S RECAP

Before getting into the finer details of buying, selling and letting properties in the UK, let's recap our overview of entering this exciting investment arena:

- Choose which type of property investment you wish to engage in – the quick flip, deeper renovation to sell, long-term buy to let.
- Research and find your location – the number one priority. Choose your area, and start from there. For the best possible chance of making a good profit on either your sale or rental, buy property in an area that is popular or widely considered 'up-and-coming'. This is crucial.
- Look for property bargains to be had, via an auction house or reliable estate agents, property clubs and local news media.

- Envisage property potential – look for properties strategically; seek those with potential to improve and extend functionality. This could mean buying a 2-bedroom, 1-bath house and turning it into a 4-bedroom, 2-bath house with an open-plan kitchen/diner.
- Take baby steps – start small with your first property and get a feel for the process and red-tape involved in the UK marketplace. Choose a mid-level property and avoid major development projects until you've got some experience.
- Obtain the services of a local agency who can do ALL of the above for you and more!

\* \* \* \* \* \* \* \* \* \*

The following chapter examines the importance of that well-known, but oh so true saying: *Location, Location, Location*, as well as how the time of year that you buy or sell a property can affect your profit margin.

# Chapter 4
# The Importance of Location & Timing

*Featuring the UK's property hotspots*

One of the most important, if not THE most important consideration when choosing which property to buy is the location. Personally, I feel this factor is more important than the type of property and even the price. Regardless of a property's size, condition, bargain price, if it's located in an area where no one wants to live or work, it won't sell. Location is key. Location is everything.

Location is usually the first box to tick when people are looking for a new home, whether they are in the market to buy or rent. Many buyers are willing to pay more for a property in their preferred location, whether it be for transport links, good schools, proximity to work, family and friends, shopping and leisure facilities. For commercial property, too, location is important – businesses need easy access for employees, deliveries, etc. It is therefore essential that you opt for property in the most desirable and sought-after locations. Bear in mind, however, the most desirable roads may not necessarily be in the most affluent of areas; it could be in an 'up-and-coming' part of town that the local council has scheduled for major regeneration in the near future. For the experienced investor, it is worth investigating, through the local councils, which areas have approved and upcoming commercial developments in progress, such as a major new shopping centre, leisure centre or a new school.

Overseas buyers are often keen to invest in the well-known big city locales that are tried and tested areas of investment. In London, for example, the boroughs of Westminster, Mayfair, Kensington and Chelsea, are perhaps the best known and most affluent of areas and as such boast a huge demand for investment, both foreign and domestic.

The most desirable areas, however, are not always the most expensive. What makes them desirable, or hotspots, is a variety of factors, including good transport links, placement within the commuter belt of a major city, as well as proximity to the usual amenities and regeneration areas. Buying in a hot spot virtually guarantees good re-sale potential and profit if buying strategically, for example, in terms of refurbishment potential.

Take, for example, the following property: an existing but empty commercial premises of 5,000 square feet compromising small shops and offices over two levels situated in zone 4 of London. The surrounding area is a mixture of commercial and residential with bus stops on the doorstep and the nearest underground station and shops about a mile away. Subject to obtaining planning permission, this property has potential for the residential development of several flats aimed at professionals working in Central London.

This is a typical example of a 'deep renovation' project that could be based in any of the UK's large cities. As discussed, you are more likely to earn higher returns if the precise location is in a well-known and sought-after area. The security of placing one's hard-earned money in a very popular area, where it is guaranteed to increase, is particularly reassuring for the overseas investor.

To recap, whether you are looking to purchase property for a long-term let or looking to 'flip' a property for a quick return, the key points to consider in terms of location are:

1. Employment
   Are there businesses in the area which offer employment to the local population, possibly your new buyers or tenants? Consider areas with universities and colleges, large-scale employers such as teaching hospitals, in which rental properties are always in demand.
2. Accessibility
   Are there good links to public transport and major road systems? This is particularly important in cities, where many people don't have cars and rely on public transport.
3. Amenities
   Is the property far from supermarkets, shops and community services, e.g. swimming pool, cinema, park, health services?
4. Good Schools
   This is vital if your property is suitable for families. Parents will pay over and above market value for a property if it means their child will have a chance at getting in to their preferred school. Find out what the catchment area is for the nearest schools – this can be a

major selling point. However, it is prudent to research the reputation of the local school also. If a property is on the doorstep of a primary or secondary school with a poor government Ofsted rating, that will be a deal-breaker for many parents.

5. Neighbours

    For residential properties, investigate who else lives in the vicinity. The UK is incredibly multi-cultural, particularly in the cities. It is good to know who the neighbours are as this may dictate who your buyer will be. If the street is a cul-de-sac with mostly senior citizens, it may not be a top choice for your young professional couple.

## UK PROPERTY HOTSPOTS

As per *The Telegraph* newspaper article of 24th May 2017, regarding research findings by Barclays Bank, the UK's top 20 Property investment hotspots were reported to be:

1. Richmond-Upon-Thames, London
2. St. Albans, Hertfordshire
3. Three Rivers, Hertfordshire
4. Camden, London

5. Westminster, London
6. Cotswold, Gloucestershire
7. Wandsworth, South West London
8. Uttlesford, Essex
9. Mole Valley, Surrey
10. Warwick
11. South Northamptonshire
12. Hertsmere, Hertfordshire
13. Waverley, Surrey
14. East Dorset
15. Elmbridge, Surrey
16. Rushcliffe, East Midlands
17. Windsor and Maidenhead, Berkshire
18. East Renfrewshire, Scotland
19. Hart, Hampshire
20. Stratford-Upon-Avon, West Midlands

If you have a map to hand, you may have noticed that at least half of the above hotspots are in and around London – falling within the 'commuter belt' of the capital.

Barclays Bank has forecast property prices in these hotspots to rise between 23% (in Stratford-Upon-Avon) and a whopping 39.1% (Richmond-Upon-Thames) by 2021.

As you can imagine, there are various factors which lead to the upwards pressure on housing prices in the areas mentioned above. These include the following:

- High earnings which create more affordability
- High business start-up and growth rate
- High employment level
- High education rate of the residents, leading to potential higher earnings
- Low or no crime rates
- Strong expected economic growth both in the local area and nationally
- An increasing rate in growth of rental levels, indicating a likely increased rate of growth in purchasing in the future

**TIMING IS EVERYTHING**

When buying property as an investment, timing of the purchase, to a degree, is an important consideration. Whether your purchase is a buy-to-let for long-term, stable income, or a flip for short-term capital growth, or both, the time of year that you buy, and eventually sell, is pertinent.

Several factors may contribute to the value of any given property, both in the short and long term. These factors can influence your decisions and strategy, requiring careful consideration as to *when* exactly to take the plunge and put in that offer to buy. Buying at the 'wrong' time could mean that you have a mortgage-heavy property on your hands much longer than you bargained for!

As an overseas investor, the task is two-fold as considerations need to be made regarding timing in the UK as well as timing relative to your own country.

Timing considerations:

a) The UK economy
What is the state of the UK economy, both at a national level as well as regionally? During a recession, property values tend to drop rapidly for the most part. For the investor, this could make for remarkable discounted buying opportunities, particularly for buy-to-let properties. Incredible deals could be had, perhaps up to 40% under the usual market value. But bear in mind your schedule. If you are looking to buy and sell quickly, a recession would not necessarily be the right time as you could have a long while to wait before a buyer comes your way. The most recent recession in

the UK, lasting from 2007-2012, saw record numbers of repossessions. If you're playing the long game, capital-earning potential is vast during an economy downturn.

b) Your home country's economy

What is the state of your own country's economy? Is it / has it been stable? Is there a big political election coming up that could affect the economy? Consider the exchange rate of your currency to GBP. If the pound has dropped recently, that could be good news for you. Has it fluctuated much over the past couple of years? Is now a good time to release funds from your home investments/bank?

c) UK interest rates

Consider the Bank of England's interest rate movements. When the nation's central bank is offering a very low base rate, there is likely to be an increase in buying and selling activity. At the time of writing (December 2017), the Bank of England's base rate is set at 0.50%.

d) Seasonal activity

Buying and selling habits vary with the seasons, affecting supply and demand. The quietest period is from October to February, when consumers tend to hold tighter to their purse strings over the hectic Christmas holiday / New Year season and vendors have other priorities. For an investor, a lower than usual bid offered a couple of days before Christmas may well be snapped up by a seller who has had little interest so far. Most people want to move in the warmer, lighter months of the year. As spring comes along and gardens start to bloom, potential buyers are awakening from their winter slumber, happy to start viewings, and those with properties to sell are gearing up for this busy season ahead. Why is summer so busy for property activity? Families with school-age children generally prefer to move at the end of the school year to avoid the stress of children changing school mid-term.

## CASE STUDY

Michael, 44, had recently been made redundant from his long-term employment of 22 years. As such he was in possession of a large redundancy sum and was in the difficult position of having to choose how best to invest his money, given the fact he was now unemployed.

After hearing about a rags-to-riches story of an old colleague through property investment, Michael was inspired to enter this arena himself. Fortunately for him, his generous redundancy money meant that he could afford to put down a deposit on a house, make a monthly mortgage payment for up to six months, as well as set aside a refurbishment budget. Michael had enough savings already to support himself and his family for the six-month period in which he chose to take on this project.

He chose his location and type of property – an unmodernised house that had potential for expansion with a vendor who was not in a property chain. Michael discovered such a property in November and made an offer far below the asking price, knowing it would likely be rejected, which is was. He sat tight until December before making another offer. This time a slightly higher offer was accepted; perhaps the vendor had become desperate to sell, perhaps he knew it was unlikely he would find another buyer over the holiday period.

The savings that Michael made by getting the lower sale price meant he could afford to renovate the property to a quality standard in time to re-sell in late spring/summer. After a six-week renovation period, the property sold in July and Michael made a clear profit (after expenses) of GBP £28,000. While not all property transactions and refurbishments run as smoothly and quickly as Michael's, it is an amazing example of how buying the right property at the right time can be incredibly lucrative.

\* \* \* \* \* \* \* \* \*

In truth, though, there really is no ideal time to purchase your new home or property investment. The timing or schedule is relative to your own personal circumstance and preference above all else. If you're buying a property for you and your family to live in, the right time is whenever it best suits your personal needs. Sometimes we have no choice but to move over a busy holiday period, in the depths of winter!

Then there are the all-important finances to consider, which are just as important as personal circumstance. If you are thinking of buying a property to let, it is prudent to consider whether potential rental income is adequate for both the short and long term. Do the numbers work for me and my situation presently? Will they work long term, and if so for how long? If the numbers show a very good return on your investment, is anything else stopping you from proceeding? If the numbers stack up, and your personal circumstance allows, then go for it!

The following chapter enters the wonderful world of how to finance your new property venture!

# Chapter 5
# Financing & Mortgages

## Options for financing and repayment

There is no getting around the fact that, to get your property investment career off the ground in the United Kingdom, or anywhere for that matter, one needs a lump sum of money to get started. Whether you are purchasing your own home or a new business venture, the minimum amount required to cover a deposit, legal fees and refurbishment expenses naturally depends on the agreed sale price of the property you are purchasing.

There are basically two ways to raise capital:

- Use your own money, whether it be from savings, an inheritance or a gift from family, for example. If you are lucky enough to be in such a situation that is ideal! Happy days! It costs you nothing and there is no interest to pay.
- The other option is to borrow money. Borrowing from a bank, private lender,

property investment syndicate, hedge fund, family members, friends or any other lending organisations. This is sometimes referred to as OPM – 'other people's money'.

I tend to recommend borrowing and would like to take you through the various options available to enable you to make an informed decision regarding which route to take. However, I am sensitive to the fact that many people prefer to avoid borrowing money at all, if possible. This preference may be due to personal, cultural or religious beliefs. In my opinion, personally, there is no harm in using a little of your own money combined with a larger portion of someone else's money – especially when it comes from a bank whose business it is to assist investors such as yourself to get on the property ladder.

For those who are fortunate enough to be able to provide a start-up sum themselves, it is still worth considering a partial loan or mortgage. Doing so, in terms of 'checks and balances', can encourage more motivation to achieve your goals. If you have a bank you need to pay back, you won't 'rest on your laurels' and take your time during the refurbishment process. You have a lender who you MUST pay back by a certain time; failure to do so could be catastrophic, perhaps resulting in the loss of your business or even your home. That pressure (in a good way) ensures you will be on top of your refurbishment/re-sale/letting schedule and budget. When investing a lot of your own money, there is a chance you could overspend because there is no outside control.

There are several methods of borrowing money for your property venture to consider:

1. **Bank loan for business purposes**
   This is readily available to investors with a clean credit history and a generally good track record both personally and professionally. Such a loan may be secured or unsecured. The downside – it may have a high setup charge.
2. **Bank overdraft**
   A fast, short-term means of raising finance. The downside – the overdraft could be 'called in' by the lender at any time.
3. **Personal loan**
   This is an unsecured bank loan of up to £15,000 and is quite easy to obtain. It differs from the 'bank loan for business purposes' in that it is intended for personal use such as purchasing a car or home appliances. Some shrewd investors do use this form of financing,

though, for a small renovation project when working towards a quick sale and a big profit margin.

4. **Credit card**

    A credit card is relatively easy to obtain; once again this money could be used as a deposit for purchasing a property or paying for refurbishments. The downside – credit cards normally have quite high interest rates.

5. **Mortgage**

    This is the most popular form of finance for property investors. As such, we shall delve deep into the world of mortgages to share with you all the options available. Even though you will probably have a property or mortgage consultant advising you on such matters, it is wise to educate yourself in the business of property finance, to help you make decisions and choices that are best for you. It is my goal to arm you with tips and insight that will enable you to venture into the property investment world with confidence, working towards your first purchase or, indeed, your multi-million-pound portfolio of properties! So, let's read on and find out more about mortgages...

## WHAT IS A MORTGAGE AND HOW DO I GET ONE?

The official definition of 'mortgage' is – an advance of money from a lender or bank, to you, for the sole purpose of purchasing a property, in which the property itself is held by the lender as security for the debt. The mortgage deeds (proof of ownership) are handed over to you by the lender only after you have redeemed or paid off the entire debt, usually over a term of 25 years.

Most home buyers in the UK purchase their properties using the mortgage system.

Ideally, as an overseas property investor, it is a lot simpler to buy property in the UK outright, using your own funds. On the other hand, if you need to or prefer to purchase a property using a mortgage from a UK bank, it is certainly possible. Naturally, though, lenders to overseas applicants have specific requirements:

1. Proof of identity – this is a regulatory requirement in the UK and this may include a passport or driving licence.
2. Proof of address – this could be a utility bill, bank statement as well as a driving licence.

3. Proof of income – in terms of affordability, the bank or lender will usually want to know about your employment or self-employment status and annual income for at least three years.
4. Proof of source of funds – for the purposes of monitoring money laundering attempts, the bank will need to know from where you obtained the deposit, e.g. from business profits or savings. This is compulsory.

Identifying the right agent or advisor, such as Timo Real Estate Solutions, is invaluable not only for guidance through the entire process of finding the best property but also for helping you select the most suitable mortgage product that is best for you based on your own circumstances.

Over the years, the mortgage market has become increasingly complex. In addition to the standard residential property mortgage described earlier, there are several different mortgage products available from a variety of lenders.

## FLEXIBLE MORTGAGES

### Advantages:

- Flexibility of payment amounts
- Daily interest
- Lower than variable interest rate
- Flexibility of payment schedule
- Able to 'draw down' / release equity
- Unlikely redemption penalty

### Disadvantage

- Large deposit required
- High set-up fees

A 'flexible mortgage' is essentially a repayment mortgage that also offers some flexibility, as the name suggests! The flexibility includes the option to make extra payments when you have extra money, or the option to reduce or possibly miss a few monthly mortgage payments completely. This can be very helpful when the unexpected happens, such as job loss or general cash-flow issues arise. For those of you who do not have a steady or consistent income, particularly people who are self-employed, a flexible mortgage is an ideal option. It allows you to pay more in a 'cash rich' month and less when in a 'cash poor' month.

The borrower can also make random lump-sum repayments to reduce the overall outstanding balance – this can reduce considerably the interest payable.

One of the main advantages of a flexible mortgage is that the interest is usually calculated daily, rather than monthly or annually (which is how most other mortgages calculate interest). When interest is calculated monthly or annually, there is a time lag before the amount you have paid is deducted from the sum owing, and therefore your interest payments are not reduced straightaway. With daily calculation of interest, the amount you pay is credited immediately – every penny acts to reduce the cost of borrowing there and then.

Making overpayments on your mortgage with some consistency can save you thousands of pounds in mortgage costs. In some cases, it is possible to pay off the mortgage much sooner, perhaps in 15 years rather than 25! I often recommend this type of mortgage whether your income is stable or inconsistent as, in the long run, you will indeed save yourself a great sum.

Another advantage: the interest rate on a flexible mortgage is often charged at a slightly lower rate than the same lender's standard variable rate. You can also choose your own payment schedule, for example a weekly or fortnightly basis, rather than monthly payments.

If you do consistently make extra repayments over a long period of time, a flexible mortgage also allows you to 'draw down' funds without needing to re-mortgage or withdraw any previous overpayments made. This means you can obtain a certain amount of cash if needed.

A flexible mortgage does not usually charge a redemption penalty if you pay off the mortgage early. This is a HUGE advantage for the property investor who is renovating and re-selling a property quickly!

Surely there must be a downside, I hear you ask! Well, yes. The disadvantage of a flexible mortgage is that it often requires a large deposit to obtain, perhaps 25% or more. A flexible mortgage also does not normally offer a fixed or discounted interest rate and the set-up administration fees could be higher than those of a standard mortgage.

## NON-STATUS MORTGAGES

**Advantage:**

- For those who don't meet status requirements

**Disadvantage:**

- High interest rate

Generally, mortgage lenders describe mortgage applications as 'status' or 'non-status'. If you meet all the lender's usual mortgage requirements you will be assigned a status mortgage. For UK residents, these conditions include: providing proof of identity and address for three years or more, full-time employment or self-employed with three years' worth of audited accounts, plus the proof of affordability and provision of property valuation checks. For overseas residents (as detailed at the beginning of this chapter), the same conditions apply PLUS you must prove the source of your funds.

Most mortgages approved and granted by lenders, to individuals for private home purchases, fall into this category.

A non-status mortgage, on the other hand, is one in which the mortgage applicant does not qualify for a status mortgage. Perhaps the applicant earns a sufficient income, regularly, but does not have evidence, e.g. payslips, to prove it. Perhaps the applicant has a poor credit history. You will be pleased to learn that some lenders may still grant a mortgage to such an applicant. A non-status mortgage is based on self-certification — this means that one simply needs to prove that he/she can afford to make the mortgage repayments. The applicant must officially and legally declare that their income is of the level disclosed; this declaration exempts the applicant from producing payslips or accounts.

This type of mortgage is not commonly approved, but it does happen. The main disadvantage of a non-status mortgage is that the interest rate will probably be higher than that of a status mortgage as the lender must consider the extra risk involved.

Although it is generally advisable to obtain a status mortgage whenever possible, do not despair if lenders decline your application. Failure to secure a status mortgage does not mean the end of your property investment career before it even begins! Non-status mortgages do exist and can be secured. During such time, take the opportunity to save some money and sort out the obstacles that have prevented you from getting a status mortgage. Turn to the *Additional Resources* chapter to learn about how to improve your credit rating if that is the issue that is preventing you from securing a status mortgage.

Also bear in mind that while one lender may offer you only a higher-charging non-status mortgage, another lender may decide to grant you a status mortgage! It is crucial that you, or your advisor, shop around all the lenders for the best mortgage for you.

## COMMERCIAL MORTGAGES

**Advantage:**

- Few restrictions on property purpose
- Larger mortgage amounts possible

**Disadvantages:**

- Slightly higher interest rates
- Fixed/discounted rates unlikely

Mortgages for the purchase of a commercial property have their own set of criteria, advantages and disadvantages. Commercial property may include shops, warehouses, factories, apartment blocks, independent schools, hotels and guest houses, and even a portfolio of houses, the list goes on...

With a commercial mortgage, the main advantage is that you have few or no restrictions on what you can do with the property you have purchased! The mortgage amount you can obtain is usually much larger than what you can secure with a residential mortgage.

The only disadvantages with a commercial mortgage are a slightly higher interest rate than that of a residential, as well as the fact that fixed or discounted rates are unlikely.

**BUY-TO-LET MORTGAGES**

A buy-to-let mortgage (BTL) is specifically granted for the purchase of a residential property solely for letting purposes rather than owner occupation. There are a variety of advantages and disadvantages to a BTL.

## Advantages:

- It is possible to have one or several mortgages on different properties, in addition to a mortgage on your own home.
- The lender will take into account the potential rental income of the property when calculating the maximum mortgage level. This means your personal income is not necessarily relevant.
- It is relatively easy to be accepted for a BTL, subject to the lender's valuation and assessment of the potential (or current) rental income. In fact, some BTL mortgage products do not even demand proof of income!
- A BTL is often more flexible than a standard mortgage; timeframes may be between 5-30 years.
- If you have a good credit history and relationship with your bank you may even be granted a mortgage amount over and above the property's worth, to finance refurbishment of the property.
- The interest rate payments on a BLT may qualify for tax relief for UK taxpayers.

## Disadvantages:

- The interest rate on a buy-to-let mortgage is usually highly than that of a standard mortgage. From the lender's point of view, you are ultimately running a business from which you are receiving rental income from the tenants occupying your property.
- Lenders often require a large deposit of at least 25% for a buy-to-let mortgage.
- A BTL can prove a hindrance as lenders may not grant you a second mortgage on your own home, should you need one, if you already have a BTL. However, if the tables are turned, having a mortgage on your own home to begin with does not affect your chances of acquiring a buy-to-let mortgage.

Interest rates for BTLs are available as fixed, variable, capped and discounted. To ensure a viable and successful rental project, it is recommended that rental income from a buy-to-let property should range between 130% and 150% of the monthly mortgage repayments.

*Important note: if you obtain a standard residential mortgage to buy a property and later decide to rent it out, you must obtain prior permission from the lender.*

## SECOND MORTGAGES (SECURED LOANS)

You may find yourself in the rather pleasant situation, one day, whereby a property you purchased long ago has appreciated in value quite dramatically and you are now sitting on a huge sum of EQUITY.

I recall the story of a client of mine to illustrate. Having purchased a 1-bedroom flat in Primrose Hill, London, for £79,000 in 1998, my client was astonished to discover the same property was worth £600,000 in 2015. With only a small mortgage remaining to pay in the next eight years, she had several hundred thousand pounds of equity on her hands! Her problem now was deciding what to do with all that equity. A nice problem to have!

My client's story certainly proves that it is worth considering the equity you have built up in your own residence, if you are currently a home owner. You may be sitting on an amazing amount of business capital, particularly if your property is in a large cosmopolitan city such as London where prices are always on the rise.

To release your equity without having to sell up is possible by obtaining a second mortgage; this is a loan secured against the property in question. If you can't repay the mortgage, the lender will seize the property and sell it to recoup their loan.

The main advantage of a second mortgage is that you don't need a flawless credit rating. However, you will pay a higher interest rate if your credit rating is poor. Generally, though, interest rates on secured loans are often much cheaper than other types of loan.

The main disadvantage of a loan being secured against your home is that you could lose it if you can't make the monthly payments. Interest rates, though often lower than others, are usually variable and could increase in time.

### REPAYMENT OPTIONS

The various mortgage types discussed so far have two things in common: they all need to be repaid in a specified period of time and they all charge interest for the privilege! There are two methods of repaying the mortgage amount to the lender: repayment and interest-only.

## REPAYMENT METHOD

This is the method whereby you repay both the capital and interest in instalments until the total sum is paid back. The monthly payments tend to be the same, subject only to interest rate change (should you choose a variable rate mortgage product). During the early years of repayment, most of the money will go towards paying off the interest, with little actually paying off the capital sum. It won't be until many years down the road that you repay the capital. This method of repayment is most suitable for property investors and entrepreneurs who are looking to buy properties to keep for the medium and long term for rental income and capital growth.

## INTEREST-ONLY METHOD

This means of paying back the loan consists of repaying monthly only the interest on the capital sum. The amount payable each month may vary, too, depending on the interest rate at the time. You do not repay any of the capital during the lifetime of the mortgage. The capital is repaid as a lump sum only at the end of the mortgage period. The upside of this mortgage type is that the monthly payments are significantly lower than those of a repayment mortgage.

If you are a private home buyer, paying only the interest means you are left with a large capital sum to repay at the end of the mortgage term – the downside of the interest-only method. In some cases, property owners may not have the means to do so! The only alternative in that unfortunate scenario is to sell up!

However, this option could be right for you, the property investor, as:

- monthly payments would be at a bare minimum while your property (or portfolio of properties) is gaining value and therefore, in theory, it would be worth more than enough to repay the mortgage in full at the end of the mortgage term.
- it is particularly useful for short-term lending as well as 'flipping' projects, whereby you don't intend on having the mortgage for a long period and will sell up long before the mortgage term has come to an end.

So how does one ensure the funds are available to pay off the capital sum when it is due? With the interest-only method, it is always advisable to marry it with a lump sum repayment vehicle, such as a life insurance policy, pension fund or some other savings scheme that is designed to repay the capital sum at the end of the mortgage period. Throughout the life of the interest-only mortgage, you are effectively making two payments: one to repay the interest and one to pay into an investment policy or account which, on maturity, aims to meet the capital sum repayment due at the end of the mortgage term.

Alternatively, you could also make lump-sum or regular overpayments on the mortgage or, in time, switch the mortgage to repayment method.

## INTEREST RATES

One of the most important considerations to make when choosing a mortgage product is the interest rate. There are several mortgage products available on the market with a variety of interest rates to meet the different requirements of property buyers.

## Variable Rate

The standard arrangement for most mortgages is the variable rate. As the name suggests, the rate varies in accordance with the activity of the Bank of England base rate. In the United Kingdom, most banks or lenders charge in the region of 1.25% above the Bank of England base rate on their own standard variable rate (SVR) mortgages. Therefore, as the base rate changes, so too will the interest you pay on your mortgage.

A variable rate can be the ideal choice for property investors as, even though the interest does vary occasionally, you will certainly know what you need to pay at the same rate relative to the base rate.

## Fixed Rate

With a fixed-rate mortgage, the interest rate is fixed regardless of the Bank of England base rate activity. The rate is fixed only for an agreed period of time – two years, five, or even 10 years. This type of mortgage rate is perfect for the first-time homebuyer as it allows one to budget with a good degree of certainty over a set term.

For property investors, the fixed rate isn't necessarily the best choice as, even though you won't pay more for your mortgage if the rate rises, you will pay more than you need to if the interest rate drops. There are also stiff penalties to pay if you wish to redeem the mortgage.

The fixed-rate mortgage is best suited to a buyer who is intending to retain ownership of the property for the medium- or long-term future. If you purchase a property with a five-year fixed-rate mortgage and plan to live there for the entire five years, then fixed rate is the way to go.

### Discounted Rate

Mortgages offering a discounted rate of interest usually guarantee that the rate you pay will always be less than the lender's standard variable rate – for a specified timeframe. For example, if the lender's standard variable mortgage rate is 5%, a discount of 2% could be offered, giving you an interest rate payable of 3%. If the lender's standard rate rises to 7% you will still receive the 2% discount, with your resulting discount rate becoming 5%.

This type of mortgage interest may not be the best choice for a property investor as it applies only for a specified time. Penalties attached to the mortgage products with discounted rates may make it difficult to transfer the mortgage to another provider. Once the time period has expired, the interest rate will usually revert to the bank's variable rate. My advice is to approach the bank at least six months prior to the current mortgage expiry date to discuss or negotiate a better rate of interest. In most cases, a competitive fixed rate is preferred.

**Capped Rate**

A capped rate is a combination of a fixed-rate and variable-rate mortgage. The rate does vary, but only between an upper cap and a lower limit. You could end up paying higher or lower than the standard rate – it all depends on which way the interest rates move. This style of mortgage rate is a great means of making budgeting easier, particularly for first-time buyers.

For property investors, too, the capped rate works well for those on a very tight budget. There are redemption penalties to consider, but they are generally lighter than those of a fixed-rate mortgage. Capped rate mortgages also offer the option to overpay and/or underpay, something we don't see with standard rates.

\* \* \* \* \* \* \* \* \*

The process of searching for the right mortgage product can be time-consuming and, at times, complicated. It is so important to do your homework and research before approaching any bank or lender to apply for a mortgage. It makes all the difference if you are knowledgeable about the options available to you. In the long run, it is certainly worth it to take the time to choose your mortgage carefully. If you are a foreign investor looking to obtain a mortgage in the UK, taking advice from a professional mortgage broker can save you time, money and simplify the whole process for you. Only choose a broker who has been highly recommended to you before entrusting him/her with your business.

Now that we have covered the financing options available, let's move forward with the fun stuff – exploring the huge array of property types to choose from!

# Chapter 6
# Residential Investment

## *Property type options*

In the United Kingdom, there is great variety when it comes to types and sizes of residential property, from the traditional Victorian houses to boutique city-slick apartments or country cottages and manors – there is something for every taste and budget. Overall there are six general residential categories that exist in the UK, each with its advantages and disadvantages: flats, detached houses, semi-detached houses, terraced houses, cottages and bungalows.

**FLAT OR APARTMENT**

A flat, or apartment, is a living area that is self-contained within a building. It is usually situated in a building that is divided up into multiple dwellings for different residents. Some are on two levels. Some are on two levels with a separate, private entrance – known as a *maisonette*. There are usually common areas, such as the main entry hall, rubbish disposal, as well as communal outside space, e.g. gardens and perhaps a carpark. In the UK flats are usually situated in towns and cities.

**Advantages:**

- You effectively have two secure front doors, one at the building's main entrance and one for your individual flat. If you are above the ground floor, security is even greater. You also have comfort in the knowledge that neighbours are nearby.
- Utilities such as electricity, gas and hot water are often supplied and regulated on a communal scale which can be cost effective.
- A large complex will probably have well-maintained gardens for use by residents.
- Some large apartment blocks provide access to health club facilities, such as a gym, tennis court or swimming pool.
- A management company will be contactable, perhaps even on the premises, to advise the services of plumbers, electricians, etc., making the maintenance of the flat as easy as possible. They are also a great help in terms of advice regarding all manner of issues relating to the property, such as rubbish and recycling collection.

- Management companies may also be able to help should you need to sub-let your flat for any reason, further enabling you to generate income from your investment with limited effort.
- The property may include a carpark. Not all apartment blocks can offer parking, but when they do, it is a godsend – especially in London! Parking spaces are usually well defined and allocated.
- If you are new to the area, with no friends or relatives nearby, purchasing or living in a flat is a great opportunity to get to know other tenants in the building.
- Blocks of flats are usually well situated in terms of amenities, such as public transport and shops.

**Disadvantages:**

- Inability to extend the property.
- Restrictions apply in terms of refurbishing the exterior of your home.
- Maintenance fees for communal areas can be high.
- There is often limited scope for gardening and pet ownership.

- For some people, the likelihood of regular contact with neighbours might be considered a negative aspect. If bad feelings arise towards a neighbour, it is difficult to avoid them!
- Walls between adjacent flats are not 100% sound proof; sound travels through floors and ceilings too. If you are an early riser and an immediate neighbour is a night owl, it could be a problem.

## TERRACED HOUSE

A terraced house is one of a long row of attached houses. They are generally identical in structure and appearance, both externally and internally in terms of layout. Terraced houses share the walls separating each property. The end-of-terrace house is exactly as the name suggests, with only one common wall. This style of housing in the United Kingdom dates back to the $17^{th}$ century, when stylish terraced townhouses were built for the nobility, particularly in the Regent's Park area of London and also regionally in towns such as Bath and Cheltenham. It wasn't until the $19^{th}$ century that terraced houses were built as low-cost housing for the urban working class of Victorian Britain.

## Advantages:

- A terraced house is relatively cheaper to buy than a semi-detached or detached property in the same area.
- There is often scope for converting the loft of a terraced house into a bedroom.
- If there is a big enough outside area in front, you could get permission to convert it to an on-site parking space.

## Disadvantages:

- Privacy is reduced, as two walls are shared with neighbours (unless end-of-terrace).
- Often terraced houses have small gardens, or only a small patio, perhaps no outside space at all.

## SEMI-DETACHED HOUSE

This style of house in the UK involves two houses sharing one wall only. Victorian semi-detached houses, built a century ago during the reign of Queen Victoria, are commonplace throughout the UK. A further boom of semi-detached dwellings rose in the 1930s in suburban developments, a symbol of middle-class aspiration.

**Advantages:**

- There is a good degree of privacy, even with one shared wall.

**Disadvantages:**

- Maintenance of your side of the property is your sole responsibility.
- Your neighbour must be considered regarding any major renovation or extension on your side. You may or may not need to get their approval, legally, before anything extensive. Either way, it is good practice to inform them and keep a friendly relationship!

## DETACHED HOUSE

As the name suggests, this type of house is not joined to another property; it is a single dwelling that does not share any walls with another building. Detached houses generally provide more privacy than terraced properties and are more expensive than any other type of house. They can range in size from a 3-bedroom suburban home to a city mansion or country manor.

**Advantages:**

- You are automatically a freeholder, rather than a leaseholder, of the property.
- Maximum privacy. A detached house is free of adjoining neighbours and includes the space surrounding the building, within the specified borders of land registry documents. Depending on local regulations, you may extend or modify your property without a permit from a lease-holding landlord.
- You don't need to pay property management/maintenance fees as you would in a block of apartments.

**Disadvantages:**

- All repairs and maintenance costs for a detached house are the sole responsibility of the owner. If you own one of four flats in a converted house, for example, the cost of any improvements, as well as maintenance, would be shared equally among the flat owners. Not so when you own the entire property yourself!

Within the category of detached houses, the UK also has bungalows and cottages.

## BUNGALOW

A bungalow is a house on one level with no stairs. A bungalow with a room in the loft is called a 'chalet bungalow'. Bungalows may be detached or semi-detached. Not to be confused with a cottage, the difference lies in the history, value and style. Bungalows are also, in general, cheaper than cottages.

This style of residence in the UK emerged due to British colonialism in India. Colonial administrators in the $19^{th}$ century adapted the classic Indian architectural style of low roofs with surrounding porches. The word 'bungalow' originates from the Hindi word 'bangla', describing the homes built for European settlers in Bengal.

### Advantages:

- It is on one level, making it ideal for elderly or disabled residents who may struggle with stairs.
- The one level has a large roof that is ideal for installing solar panels, which always add value.
- Being on one level makes maintenance jobs easier to complete, such as cleaning windows and gutters.

- There are increased options for altering room usage, e.g. changing a dining room into a bedroom.

**Disadvantages:**

- Less efficient heating as the ground floor bedrooms do not benefit from heating via rooms that would otherwise be underneath them.
- They take up more land; a 2-bedroom bungalow may cover the same size plot as a 4-bedroom multi-level terraced house.

**COTTAGE**

The quintessentially British countryside home is undoubtedly the cottage. Purposely built with thick walls to withstand the cold British winters, they usually have small windows, low ceilings, and the most traditional style boasts a thatched roof. Modern cottages usually have two levels, with the top floor smaller than the ground. Originally built in rural or semi-rural locations, some cottages have since been developed in cities. Historically, these homes date back as far as the Middle Ages, when they were built to house farm workers and their families on the estates of feudal landlords. Since then, the 'quaint cottage' style has been greatly sought after and is reflected in the price.

## Advantages

- Older cottages retain a lot of character and charm.
- They are good for an extra source of income if let as a holiday home; perfect for your own family holiday when not occupied!

## Disadvantages

- Cottages tend to have quite low ceilings.
- Small windows mean the rooms may not get a lot of natural light.

## OTHER OPTIONS

## Retirement Properties

UK retirement properties are built purposely for those of us over 55 years of age. They are usually secure blocks of apartments, sometimes set within gated communities, that offer a wide range of amenities catering for senior citizens.

## Advantages

- They are usually located within walking distance of local amenities.
- An in-house support system including assistance alarms.
- Organised social activities for residents.
- The premises are highly secure.
- They hold their value as there is usually less wear and tear created by residents.

## Disadvantages

- Although the market is growing rapidly, it is a niche market with limited appeal.
- Maintenance charges imposed are usually quite high.

## New Builds / Off-Plan Property Investments

Across the United Kingdom, there are thousands of flats and houses that are built daily for residential accommodation. Let's face it… all of us humans must have shelter or a place we call home, where we sleep, and our own territory in which to relax. For most of us, one would usually get a good job with a salary that would enable us to buy a home for the family.

A property investor, on the other hand, who may want to build a property portfolio, should seriously consider buying new build as well as off-plan flats or houses. This is a very big market in the UK and there are various mortgage products as well as government incentives available on the market for investors and first-time buyers respectively.

The pros of buying these new build properties include high potential for equity growth from day one, a 10-year NHBC (National House-Building Council) warranty covering any structural defects, no chain and the possibility of choosing the fixtures and finishes to the property as it is being built. The possible cons, on the other hand, may vary from delays on completing the property construction in good time as well as building defects and, in some cases, poor quality on completion.

\* \* \* \* \* \* \* \* \* \*

Now that we've covered the options available for investing in residential property, let's turn to the following chapter, detailing all the options that are out there when it comes to commercial property investment.

# Chapter 7
# Commercial Investment

## *Choices and use classes*

Like residential properties, commercial premises come in a variety of shapes and sizes. While the only purpose of a residential property is to provide a home, commercial buildings are flexible in that they can provide premises for a variety of businesses, including retail premises, warehouses, factories, hotels, hostels, care homes, offices, nightclubs, petrol stations, restaurants, car showrooms, garages, sports facilities, shopping centres, distribution centres, storage facilities, private schools and hospitals, to mention but a few.

We at Timo Real Estate Solutions are in a great position to help you to identify the ideal commercial property investment for you and, most importantly, at a very discounted or reduced price. We manage to achieve this because of our great negotiation skills coupled with the broad knowledge and experience of the UK Commercial Property market.

Our friends at the Knight Frank real estate consultancy have undertaken research into the habits and preferences of their commercial investors, revealing some interesting results. When respondents were asked why they chose commercial real estate, most stated that diversification of their property portfolio was a key reason, as well as the welcome stability of long-term rentals as an ongoing income stream. There was a distinct preference for 'core' investments, such as centrally based offices and retail units in metropolitan areas. Knight Frank also reported that Central London was still a popular destination for overseas property investment with the commercial office market alone attracting over £9.3 billion worth of deals by foreign buyers. With the pound falling in the aftermath of the Brexit vote, the momentum is expected to continue.

For investors interested in buying, leasing or renting commercial property, please note there is legislation in place that dictates permissible uses. In the UK, the Town and Country Planning (Use Classes) Order of 1987 defines the possible uses of a site, with 'site' meaning "the whole area of land within a single unit of occupation." The vast majority of property in the

United Kingdom will have had its permissible uses already assigned by the relevant local authority.

## THE USE CLASSES

The classes of potential uses are divided into categories. For example, the use classes falling under Part A are types of professional service provided to the public and business communities, including the sale of goods or service in shops. The main categories are further divided into subgroups, each of which contains the specific uses with which the law is actually concerned. Each of the subgroups is assigned a letter from A to D and a number, creating for example a 'Class A1 Use', a 'Class B3 Use', etc.

The Local Planning Authority uses each class to enable them to create a suitable balance between residential neighbourhoods and areas for business purposes. They have the authority to effectively prohibit a use which would be inappropriate due to a particular property's location or other relevant considerations. The aim is to prevent any type of business activity taking place which would have a detrimental effect on the local community. For example, the local authority would certainly not allow the operation of an abattoir, or a cocktail bar, next to a school or block of flats.

Briefly, the property classes of use are as follows:

## Class A – Shops (including some services)

This category is further subdivided into a variety of everyday commercial uses.

## Class A1 – Shops and retail outlets

The criteria here is that all potential customers will be "visiting members of the general public." Commercial property in this class may include:

- Shops (where goods are sold)
- Post offices
- Premises where tickets are sold and travel agents
- Premises selling cold food (intended for consumption offsite)
- Hairdressers
- Florists
- Funeral directors
- Premises where goods for sale are displayed
- Premises from which "domestic or personal" goods or services are hired
- Premises where articles are deposited for washing, cleaning or repair

## Class A2 – Professional services

Class A2 moves on to cover "financial and professional services" offered to the general public. The specification is that visitors to the premises will be clients or customers of these types of businesses.

- Financial services
- Professional services (excluding health or medical services)
- Any other services deemed appropriate for location within a shopping area

## Class A3 – Food and drink

There is only use permitted for Class A3 premises – the sale of "food and drink", either to be consumed on site, or on or offsite in the case of hot food.

## Class A4 – Drinking establishments

Class A4 establishments include public houses, pubs and bars.

## Class A5 – Hot food and takeaway

For businesses selling hot food intended for consumption off the premises.

## Class B – Further business and industrial activities

This class covers all sorts of common business activities and is prefaced by the provision "for all or any of" the activities described in Class B1. Further B classes relate increasingly to specific industrial processes.

## Class B1 – Business

Offices, excluding those already mentioned within Class A2.

- Premises for research and development
- Industrial processes which are permitted to take place within a residential area without damaging the "amenity of that area."

It is recommended you seek professional guidance before proceeding with negotiations to occupy commercial premises as the use classes are quite generalized.

## Class B2

This class refers to facilities for general industrial use, for example, carrying on an industrial process which does not fall within class B1 or within classes B3 to B7.

Such businesses might include a textile manufacturing company, a production and sales facility of an electronics manufacturer or a warehouse for miscellaneous storage and distribution services.

### Class B3 – Special industrial group A

Class B3 relates to activities which must be registered according to the Alkali, Etc. Works Regulation Act 1906. The only exceptions are those activities which come under classes B4 through B7, and are therefore assigned to Special Industrial Group B.

### Class B4 – Special industrial group B

This class pertains to specific types of metal works, although not those carried out in a quarry or mine (or adjacent to one).

### Class B5 – Special industrial group C

This includes works involving heavy industrial processing of minerals, again excluding quarries or mines. Some examples here are "producing rubber from scrap," "boiling or running linoleum gum," and "manufacturing acetylene from calcium carbide."

## Class B6 – Special industrial group D

This special industrial group deals with activities involving work with oils, gums, resins, and some other types of chemical compounds. The first entry in this class makes it clear that petroleum and petroleum products are not included.

## Class B7 – Special industrial group E

This group includes processes for materials of animal origin and includes 14 different uses. Class uses range from processing potential food stuffs such as the boiling or cleaning of tripe or curing fish to more general processes involving animal products. An example here is producing manure or processing animal skins, such as leather.

## Class B8 – Special industrial group F

This class covers warehouses and the like, applying to properties which are used "for storage or as a distribution centre."

## Class C – Hotels, hostels and dwelling houses

### Class C1

C1 is provided for dwellings where no significant element of care is provided. These include hotels, guest houses or hostels.

### Class C2

Class C2 covers the following types of premises, providing they include residential facilities:

- Hospitals and nursing homes
- Schools, colleges or training centres

### Class C3

This class covers the business of a 'dwelling house' as a principal or secondary residence. It comprises three sub-categories:

**C3 (a)** Refers to one or more people living together as a single household as defined by the Housing Act 2004; what could be construed as a 'family'.

**C3 (b)**: Refers to a group of up to six people living together as a single household and receiving care, e.g.

supported housing schemes such as those for people with learning disabilities or mental health problems.

**C3 (c)** This allows for groups of up to six people living together as a single household. C3 (c) allows for those groupings that do not fall within the C4 HMO definition, but which fit within the previous C3 use class, to be provided for, i.e. a small religious community may fall into this section as could a homeowner who rents out a room to a lodger.

## Class C4

**Houses in multiple occupations** (also known as a house share). Class C4 includes small shared houses occupied by three to six unrelated individuals as their only or main residence, and who share basic amenities such as a kitchen or bathroom.

In situations where more than six people are sharing a large house, such multiple occupation is unclassified by the Use Classes Order. In planning terms, such properties are described as being *sui generis*. In this case, a planning application will be required for a change of use from a dwelling house to a large house in multiple occupations or from a Class C4 house in multiple occupations to a large house in multiple occupations where a material change of use is considered to have taken place.

## Class D – Non-residential institutions

### Class D1

This class takes into consideration the many public services which do not seem to fall under Class A:

- Medical or health services premises which don't form a part of the practitioner's home
- Crèches, day nurseries or day centres
- Premises for education
- Premises which display works of art without commercial transactions (sale or hire)
- Museums
- Public libraries or reading rooms
- Public or exhibition halls
- Premises "for, or in connection with, public worship or religious instruction"

## Class D2

This class covers the use of premises for entertainment and leisure purposes:

- Cinemas
- Concert halls
- Bingo halls or casinos
- Dance halls
- Swimming pools, ice skating rinks, gymnasiums or an "area for other indoor or outdoor sports or recreations, not involving motorised vehicles or firearms"

## Sui generis

Certain uses do not fall within any use class and are considered *sui generis*. Such uses include: theatres, houses in multiple occupation, hostels providing no significant element of care, and scrap yards. Others include petrol stations and shops selling or displaying motor vehicles, retail warehouse clubs, nightclubs, launderettes, taxi businesses, amusement centres and casinos.

\* \* \* \* \* \* \* \* \*

Now let's venture into the exciting world of land development — potentially the most lucrative and creative field of property investment you can enter!

# Chapter 8
# Land & Other Development Options

*Plot potential, how to develop, asset stripping and more*

Opportunities for investing in property are varied, there isn't just one rigid custom of how to do it. Ranging from the short-term 'quick flips' to the long-term investments sitting nicely to bestow to one's children, there is something for everyone in the property arena. The most popular avenues for property investment in the UK include:

- Purchasing a property at the lowest price possible (of course!), renovating it to add value, such as loft conversion for an extra bedroom, new bathrooms, an extension for an open-plan kitchen, landscaping, etc.
- Purchasing an auction-house property at a very low price and selling it on in a matter of weeks, months or years. This may or may not require major renovations (or perhaps just paintwork and a tidy up).

- Gradually building up a portfolio of rental properties, earning passive income via your tenants on a weekly, monthly or annual basis. This long-term option is a great way to earn a steady income that, after the initial purchase and refurbishment, requires little demand on your time, particularly if you have an agent to manage the tenancies and building maintenance.
- Apply all the above suggestions to commercial property too! Bear in mind that commercial lettings can often be secured with very long leases of five years or more.

In addition to the above, one might call, safer options, there are other opportunities for lucrative investment projects. One of the more rewarding options, although somewhat riskier, is land development.

If you are determined to make big money through property investment, then land development is the route to take. As such, I have devoted a lot of pages to this topic. There is much to consider and knowledge is power, after all!

Land development involves sourcing plots of unused land and transforming them into building plots which are worth far more than the original land once housing is built. The fact that land with a building on it is far more valuable than an empty space, is why land development can be the most lucrative of property investments, even for the most inexperienced developer. This brief outline of the land development business may make the process sound easy. In theory, it is a straightforward process. In reality, though, it takes a great deal of courage, vision, drive, hard work, an initial amount of capital, plus skilled and reliable professionals, to see such a project through from start to finish.

Step one: find a plot of land for sale... and execute your building plans! This is property development on the grandest scale. There are plenty of plots of land throughout the United Kingdom offering great potential for building a new residence from the ground up, be it one or more detached houses or a block of flats. Don't forget the commercial route too, by building units for office space or warehousing, for example. How about a 'half and half', mixed-use premises – a ground floor build of office units with residential apartments on top? Read on for further details and suggestions regarding all these options.

Land development can certainly be a gold mine. However, the perfect plot may be hard to find as you need to be clear and strict in your purpose for the intended build. If you do your homework, investigate all the options in terms of land use permissions from the local authorities, when the right plot comes along in the right location, at the right price, you could find yourself with a massive profit at the end of the development! It is perfectly feasible that one major land development project per year could net you a profit of several hundred thousand pounds.

As mentioned previously, in the UK, there is the sticky issue of planning permission to consider when dealing with land developments. The process of securing planning permission from the local council can be a daunting experience, especially if you are new to the property development game. It can be a lengthy period awaiting your permission, it may be rejected and you may have to revise and resubmit your plans all over again. But remember, if buying and developing land was easy then everyone would do it and everyone would be super rich! Truthfully, this speciality of property investment takes vision, courage and drive. There is certainly a level of risk involved and strategic planning is key to making the right choices, from purchasing the right plot and determining and calculating your plans for it, to ensuring you prepare a realistic schedule and budget that is ready to absorb the unexpected.

Among life's greatest rewards is reaping the fruits of your labour. A well-executed land development project entails great labour, and is sure to bear great fruit both in terms of financial gain as well as job satisfaction.

With land development, the key to success is to identify and purchase a plot with great potential for a specific use which, when developed, you can sell on for a seriously big profit. Traditionally, with the UK's chronic housing shortage, plot development into a block of apartments has always been a popular choice for investors and will undoubtedly make a decent return on one's investment. If you have the courage do so, there are more complex, and therefore more lucrative, projects out there if you are prepared to invest more money and more time.

## Plots of land in the UK with the most potential for lucrative development include the following:

- Sites with conflicting use, such as an abandoned house or derelict factory near a residential area. Purchasing an empty property and obtaining planning permission to erect residences in its place could be extremely profitable indeed. This type of development may be quite time-consuming, it is certainly not a quick-turnaround option, but the financial rewards at the end of the day could be well worth it.
- Sites in a strategic location. For residential purposes, it must be in a location where people can and want to make a comfortable and pleasant home for themselves. There needs to be easy access to various amenities – transport links, shops, schools, restaurants, entertainment and leisure facilities. If not, you may have to consider the commercial route, with a view to developing shops, offices, warehouses, etc. A good location is always in demand and is therefore a major selling point. Like any property, prices are always higher for those near good amenities.

- Sites that have a flat landscape are hard to find but are often a land developer's ideal plot. If you find one, grab it! Flat landscapes, naturally, are easier to build on and so will save you time and money that would otherwise be spent levelling out the ground.

If you choose to go down the route of land development, it is certainly worth considering using the services of agencies that specialise in sourcing such plots for property developers, to ensure you find the best plot of land for your project. Especially as a newcomer to this type of property investment, it would be well worth the commission charged if the agent can find you a most suitable plot that meets your needs, in terms of both personal preference and, also, the all-important budget.

Land-sourcing agents are well-connected in their field and offer great knowledge of local areas. They are often familiar with potential plots and their owners before the properties are even put on the market. Particularly for your first land development deal, using an agent is highly recommended.

## HOW TO DEVELOP YOUR LAND

Build Homes – the plot could be used for building houses or flats. This is the most common type of land development. There is a great demand in the UK for more housing, particularly in cities, as the population grows and migrants seek work here. Whether it be a small estate of attached and detached houses or a large apartment block, the demand is there and it's increasing.

Build Commercial Premises – such as units for shops, offices, factories, warehouses. Research the area to find out if there is any demand for commercial premises. Is there a large business park nearby but few food outlets? You could provide much-needed cafés and takeaways, which could bring in rental income for the long term. Are there many schools in the area but the local leisure centre is lacking? These days, in the UK, there is a popular trend for giant indoor trampoline parks for kids (and adults). If the location is right (near a train station or shopping district) and parking is limited, a public multi-storey carpark would be a gold mine (with no building, as such, required at all!).

Mixed Premises — a combination of residential and commercial is common nowadays in towns and cities. Perhaps you have row of shops on the ground floor (hair salon, newsagent, café) with residential apartments above, plus underground parking. Such developments provide a range of on-going income streams.

## OTHER CONSIDERATIONS

### The Local Authority's Development Plan

It is important to find out and consider the official status of the land within the local authority's development plan. Some property developers do not adhere to local planning policy, but I do not personally recommend such action. Life is much easier when you obey local authority policy and work with their community plan! It is very much worth taking the time to familiarise yourself with the relevant council's development plans to enable you to make an informed decision regarding the type of development you wish to pursue for your desired plot of land.

### Budget and Returns

As with any property investment, these are the key considerations in land development and therefore I can't stress and mention them enough! Obviously, it is vital to choose a development option that you can afford to pursue and that will provide you with a big enough profit margin to make the project worthwhile. To that end, I always recommend having a supportive team of advisors to guide you in making the best decisions for your situation. It is worth cultivating relationships with planning consultants, architects, surveyors, builders, solicitors, bank managers – that's quite a Christmas card list!

## Partnering

If you have found the ideal plot of land, have a great vision for it, but simply cannot raise the required finance, all is not lost. It may be possible to set up a partnership with the land owner. Your approach here must be carefully planned. Prepare a comprehensive development proposal to present to the owner and request a meeting in person to discuss your ideas fully. It may mean a long wait for the owner to take advice and make a decision, but that is their right and shows they are seriously considering the proposal. If luck is on your side and the owner agrees, both of you could be looking at a fruitful relationship that works for you both. There is no reason this sort of approach to development shouldn't be your preferred strategy

– taking on a development partner reduces the stress on the individual investor and it also means you may be able to take on bigger projects as you're not shouldering the burden of fully financing it.

## Purchase Before Disclosure

Another crucial consideration to achieve a profitable and efficient land development is to ensure you have a purchase agreement in place *before* disclosing your development plans. Bear in mind, the trigger for increasing the value of any land plot is the official grant of planning consent by the local authority (not the development itself). Therefore, if you do not have the right of ownership prior to commencing planning application, there is a real risk that another party could seek that permission ahead of you!

Some land developers, those happy to take great risks, actually undertake 'blind developments', whereby they apply for planning permission without having even made an offer to purchase the land (until later in the process). The risk here is that the land owner could decide, if willing and able, to proceed with development themselves, and in doing so our 'blind developer' is left out of pocket, having paid planning administration fees.

Too much work involved, you say? There is another way to go – obtain only the planning permission and then sell the plot, without doing a spot of building work. You are still likely to make a decent profit taking this route.

## FURTHER OPTIONS

Wait – there's more! As you gain development experience, there may come a time when you seek something bigger or more challenging. Land development is the epitome of 'building from the ground up' of course, but there are still other ways to satisfy your increasing development aspirations.

Discovering ownership of vacant properties and plots of land is a great challenge for those who like doing some investigation work, while asset stripping, perhaps, is land development at its most complex.

## ASSET STRIPPING

Another avenue for investing in property with a view to making 'big money' is a technique known 'ethical asset stripping'. This type of development involves more complex properties such as large farms or country estates and converting some or all their buildings into sought-after residences.

This is an adventurous method commonly used by experienced and successful investors for properties that no one else really wants – such projects are not for the faint-hearted! In so doing, it is possible to purchase a property that is much greater or expensive than one desires or could afford to develop. If the price is right, an investor can sell off carefully selected smaller parts of the estate, which, effectively, will finance the development of the remainder of the property.

A prime example of asset stripping can be related to a large farm, whereby land and several outbuildings comprise the entire property and as such can be subdivided. When buying a property that is greater than you need, your number one priority should be to sell off as soon as possible the portions you neither require nor want. You will most likely need to stretch your finances up front to secure the purchase in the first place, but careful buying and shrewd asset stripping could result in an amazing property at a well-below market rate.

When purchasing a large estate with a lot of land and outbuildings, it is common practice to consider selling various parts to recoup some of the overall expense.

Should you wish to do so, bear in mind the following factors:

- Issues such as access for builders' vehicles, planning permission, availability of utilities.
- Have an adequate nest egg of capital, just in case the segments you wish to shift first don't sell. If it's possible to do so, rent out the smaller buildings/land while they remain on the market. Another investor may prefer to buy with tenants already in place.

There are specialist property brokers in the UK who can find and bring together the various parties involved in asset stripping. It takes quite some logistical skill to find a vendor with a suitable property to satisfy someone looking to rent agricultural land, someone looking to buy outbuildings for development but not the adjoining land, and someone else wanting to buy only the main house. It is the broker's job to negotiate a compromise beneficial to all parties concerned.

### CLAIMING VACANT PROPERTIES AND LAND

We've all noticed derelict properties and empty land from time to time over the years, perhaps wondering who owns it or who once lived there. You may be surprised to learn that it is entirely possible that such a property is available to buy.

If you spot a vacant piece of land that is seemingly disused (whether it be rural, agricultural land or a derelict, overgrown city plot) there is nothing stopping you from investigating the ownership of the plot with the council, approaching the owner and asking if they wish to sell.

Be prepared to put in a great deal of effort and investigation, contacting all the relevant departments within the local council, land registry and even the local library, to discover the identity and contact details of the property's owner. Your best bet is to use a reliable property solicitor to make the necessary enquiries on your behalf. You may get a hard "No," but there is no harm in asking. You may get lucky, though, and discover the owner has been thinking about selling. By taking you up on your interest, the vendor could potentially save thousands of pounds on estate agent fees, so you, in turn, would be in a strong position to negotiate a below-market value price!

It can be a challenging exercise and, also, a frustrating one. You may find that out of a dozen properties researched only one or two turn out to be viable investment opportunities, for a variety of reasons. It's not unusual to discover and contact the owners of a derelict property, to find out they are family members who have inherited a relative's home some time ago. They intend to refurbish the property, one day, but just haven't made the time to execute any of these great plans. Hence the property has sat empty and neglected for years, sometimes decades. In this situation, it's fine to leave them your details and perhaps send an email now and then, to gently remind them of your interest! You never know when the owners may one day wake up and just want to get rid of it! The reward for your tireless persistence (without becoming annoying of course!) of trying to persuade the owner to sell, may be that you are able to buy the property at a reduced price. Once you are the new owner, have obtained your long-awaited planning permission to convert the derelict house into a block of stylish modern flats, you can reflect on the great effort that led you there! There's no reason why you couldn't develop such a property similarly to Mr Nelson in our previous case study, and end up equally successful.

Having identified a plot of underused or vacant land, and its ownership, you will be able to find out if any planning permission has been sought. If not, the land could be worth very little, depending on its location. If the same plot does have planning permission to build, it will be worth much more. Any piece of land, in a desirable location, with approved planning permission for residential building, would be worth a vast sum.

A lot can be done with a large plot of land – and you don't even have to renovate or build a thing! Let's start with subdividing the land into small plots. Apply to the local authority for permission to build on them. Then sell the individual plots to a builder or another developer for a nice profit. You don't even have to subdivide the land to resell. Just getting planning permission to build is enough of a bonus to warrant a higher re-sale value. Alternatively, if you have the time and the funds, you could build on the individual plots yourself, re-selling upon completion. This is the riskier approach for sure as, with any full development project, the longer and mostly costly it is the greater the chance for delays and issues to arise.

However, when such risk and hard work pays off, the profit is often tremendous! You may be familiar with a local plot of land that has been vacant for some time.

It is entirely possible that you could buy and develop that plot. There could be a variety of reasons for vacancy, and with some hard investigation, you may come across an amazing opportunity for a prosperous investment. Consider even, your own property. Do you have a large piece of land that could be split and sold off? Could you build on that extra space you don't really need?

\* \* \* \* \* \* \* \* \*

In the following chapter, we investigate the concept of wealth diversification – a creative investment technique of spreading your risk to achieve maximum returns.

# Chapter 9
# Wealth Diversification Tactics

*Spreading risk for maximum returns*

In the world of financial investment, the term 'diversification' is a well-known strategy many consider to be the cornerstone of a strong investment portfolio. As the name suggests, it involves making several different investments (particularly stocks and shares as well as a property portfolio) to spread out the risk of fluctuating values; it's the classic metaphor of not putting all your eggs in one basket.

There is, however, much more to investment or wealth diversification than just owning a lot of different shares. Owning stocks in several different European banks, for example, is not necessarily diversification. Owning stocks in several different gold mining corporations is not diversification. True wealth diversification is the strategic spreading of funds across several asset classes (groups of similar assets).

But it goes even further. Different asset classes perform differently, in varying cycles, offering different levels of risk.

The strategic spreading (in terms of company shares) for strong wealth diversification should be across a variety of economic sectors. Such spreading will help to ensure that, should any of those share prices drop drastically and/or a company 'goes bust', your investment portfolio won't totally collapse. The investments that are doing well protect you against the decreased values of those that unexpectedly aren't doing so well.

Strategic spreading, for example, means investments are not all in big-time international corporations. The key is to invest in different asset classes. If the stock market crashes, the other asset classes can rise. So, in addition to the high-end stocks, you may have a selection of carefully chosen small-fry stock, a mix of foreign and domestic stocks, a mix of foreign and domestic bonds, and a mix of . . . Real Estate investments. Ah, now I've caught your attention – the same principles for financial investment diversification can be applied to property – Real Estate Wealth Diversification!

## PROPERTY DIVERSIFICATION STRATEGY

Investing in a variety of properties in carefully chosen parts of the UK will balance your risk as well as your income/capital growth ratio – this is Real Estate Wealth Diversification, or, in other words, quite simply, strong, balanced property portfolio management. It is certainly a must-have strategy for the long-term investor. While property values are nowhere near as volatile as some stocks and shares, there can be fluctuations in the market, you may have unexpected issues with your property renovation projects or land developments, you may have personal financial issues unrelated to your properties, perhaps matrimonial problems, including divorce settlement. As you may be aware, anything can happen in life unexpectedly. Often times, it is not due to our own making and worse still, the circumstances may be out of our control! Diversification of your property portfolio will help to protect you against such eventualities.

Different avenues of property investment have pros and cons when it comes to risk and reward. In general terms, the principles of a strategic diversification of property investments is the practice of spreading capital according to property type, sector and location, with investments primarily in metropolitan areas.

Considerations when it comes to choosing a property type depend on usage/function (e.g. residential or commercial, and category thereof), quality of the building and investment goals (say buy-to-sell for quick return through refurbishment or long-term rental for steady income and capital growth).

Another aspect of diversification to consider is the liquidity of assets. A portion of property within the portfolio should provide some easy-access liquidity should the unexpected happen. For example, this might include steady and available cash from a long-standing rental asset. Is there a property in the portfolio that could be sold easily and quickly at any time to rescue another development project? If the optimum sales price is not achieved, though, how would that affect the overall portfolio? Could you afford to sell at a lower price than originally anticipated?

A steady income from rent is vital to the overall profitability of a diversified portfolio. Particularly attractive to investors for this reason is the commercial property sector: offices, retail units, warehouse and distribution centres, hotels, residential and nursing/care homes – businesses from which you can agree major long-term lease or rental agreements (not just the usual 12-month terms that a regular block of flats would provide). Even so, individual residential rentals are still a great diversifier as the demand isn't determined by other asset performances such as retail sales would be for a shop rental. As a matter of fact, everyone needs a home! Residential rental properties can act as a safe bet against more risky projects such as a high-end residential refurbishment. Purpose-built flats aimed at the student market in a university town, for example, is a sector which has grown steadily over the years offering relatively low risk with steady income – a classic example of the right sector in the right location.

Land development projects, requiring more capital to get off the ground, are more speculative in terms of leasing/rental potential and as such are riskier – but potentially they could be the most lucrative component of your portfolio. Your steady income, less risky portfolio investments will help protect you until you hit the jackpot with a major development opportunity!

Areas throughout the UK undergoing regeneration and improvements to infrastructure can transform a town, attracting new employers, residents and tourists. In turn, neighbouring areas can benefit in the years that follow, resulting in rising property values. The commuter belt area surrounding London is a prime example of how rising property values can spread. As prices rise higher and higher in London, more and more people are pushed to the outlying boroughs and surrounding counties, boosting demand in these areas.

## INTERNATIONAL DIVERSIFICATION

Most investors are aware of the importance of portfolio diversification, but when it comes to property portfolio management, many still favour their home country, perhaps thinking it is the least risky option. I would argue that the best opportunities for wealth diversification lie in international property investment. Property cycles can vary globally; while it may be a seller's market in your home country, the reverse could be true in London, Berlin or Singapore. Therefore, investing in property overseas is, in itself, a means of wealth diversification. By investing in properties internationally, as well as in your home country, you are diversifying. If the British pound drops at all, as it did upon news of Brexit, it can instigate good buying opportunities for foreign investors, particularly for those able to purchase high-end properties in prime London boroughs such as Kensington & Chelsea or Westminster.

## LONDON AND BEYOND

London is a long-standing property investment haven; it has the key characteristics required for a city of lucrative property opportunities: it has a diverse economy, skilled and multi-cultural labour force, good infrastructure, pro-active local government, plus extensive retail and leisure sectors. However, in recent years, other major UK cities and regions have come to the fore as property hotspots with immense potential.

While the UK is relatively a small geographical area compared to other countries of the world, it has plenty of cities with thriving development and rental opportunities. The main advantage of going outside London is that prices are generally much cheaper once you emerge outside the commuter belt. That is not to say that everywhere outside London is cheap – not at all! There are several high-end residential and commercial areas that attract a lot of foreign investment, particularly from China and the Middle East.

England's second city, Manchester, should be top of the list for regional investment beyond London. Considered the unofficial capital of the North, at the time of writing it is undergoing tremendous billion-pound regeneration projects. Nearby Liverpool, too, is undergoing development by investors from China in particular in the both commercial property realm in terms of entertainment facilities, bars and restaurants, as well as residential property.

## COMPONENTS OF A WELL-DIVERSIFIED PORTFOLIO

So what, exactly, should my portfolio consist of to ensure good diversification?

1. A range of property types / asset classes at different price points, including buy-to-sell homes, mixed use properties, HMO (House of Multiple Occupancies), with both quick flip and large renovation projects.
2. A variety of commercial premises and land development, property investment syndicates and funds.

3. Invest in different regions. London may well be your dream, but to expand your wealth diversification then you need to invest outside the capital as well.
4. A high percentage of rental income, both residential and commercial, to balance out cyclical capital growth. Include some commercial property, for which you can secure long-term leases of 5-10 years with financially stable tenants.

\* \* \* \* \* \* \* \* \*

We will dig deeper into the mechanics of the above types of portfolio investments throughout this book. Turn to the next chapter, *Building Your Portfolio*, to find out more.

# Chapter 10
# Building Your Portfolio

*Assessing risk and strategy, plus flip tips and how to break barriers*

In the previous chapters, we've discussed the basics of how, when, where and why to invest in the property market in the United Kingdom. The opportunities really are endless. In this chapter, we are going to examine the variety of investment opportunities more closely, and discuss how, with specific examples, to make shrewd property choices for creating wealth diversification both in the short and long term.

First, let's recap our basic property investment strategies:

- Buy to Sell Quickly – buy a property that needs refurbishment; this can range from a quick flip, which may be renovated in less than six months and include updating a kitchen, bathroom, paintwork, lighting… to a major renovation (entailing the aforementioned plus

room extensions, loft conversions, and the like).
- Buy to Sell 'One Day' – by a property that may or may not need renovation; location may be in an area predicted to be up and coming in a few years' time; live in it or rent it out.
- Buy to Let – purchase a property (which may or may not require refurbishment) with the intention of renting it out for immediate income as well as long-term capital growth. Consider both a mixed residential and commercial property portfolio, with shops, offices, as well as homes – a great income stream that could provide a substantial pension in retirement.
- Land Development – buy land (with or without a property on it) with potential to develop in a variety of ways before selling on or letting. Refer to the *Land & Other Development Options* chapter for extensive discussion on this highly profitable avenue for investors.

## RISK ASSESSMENT

With renovation projects that you aim to complete in the relative short term, for immediate sale, there is an element of risk. There may be times when, for a variety of reasons, a project takes much longer than originally anticipated... such as costly and unexpected repairs (wood rot, poor electrical and plumbing, rising damp, asbestos discovery, for example – albeit much of these should be discovered at survey stage), a slow or unreliable builder or weather issues disrupting exterior renovations. Particularly if you have a mortgage on the property, rather than having bought for cash, each month that passes is another payment to the bank! This will all contribute to the reduction of your profit margin.

To lessen the risk, it is imperative to choose the right property for a swift turn around to re-sell. How do we do that? Choose a property that meets the following criteria:

- A location that is desirable NOW, or at least clearly gaining in popularity (not one that is predicted to be up and coming in five years).
- A smaller property with potential for expansion or extension; avoid large properties which have a smaller target buyer in the market
- Is not a specialised property such as a barn conversion, thatched cottage, which can be

difficult to appraise and as such may affect your profit margin.
- Not a risk taker? Go for long-term rental and capital growth and choose property that meets the following criteria:
    - for immediate rentals, ensure location is amenable and popular
    - for long-term capital growth, opt for an up-and-coming location, as well as renovation/expansion potential.

**BUYING-TO-SELL QUICKLY: TOP TIPS**

1. Avoid property chains if possible. Anyone in a chain can pull out, at any time (prior to exchange of contracts). This can slow down, or even halt, your buy-to-sell process, leaving you vulnerable to fluctuations in the market. Timing is key!
2. Buy from an auction house for the best bargains and guaranteed swift completion (up to 28 days maximum), enabling you to plan ahead for your re-sale with a good degree of accuracy.
3. Whenever possible, pay by cash, saving you money on financing charges as well as a lot of time!

## CRITERIA CHECKLIST FOR BUY-TO-SELL QUICKLY

While your property may not meet all the following criteria to be a swift and lucrative investment, it should, ideally, meet most of them to give you the greatest chance of success. Does your potential property...

- Have potential for extension or conversion? Adding a bedroom, extra bathroom or dining area to small property will increase its value dramatically. Providing one of these additions can be completed in a matter of weeks for a 'quick flip'.
- Require modernisation? Perhaps the property of an elderly resident who has lived there for decades and not updated it in terms of kitchen, bathroom, electrics, heating system, etc.
- Require general maintenance and tidying up / decorative improvements; landscaping?
- Have a large plot / spare land? Is there space to add off-street parking or, better still, build another house? You could strip down the land, get planning permission to build, then sell it as is. Alternatively, build the second house yourself and sell for an even greater profit!

- Have a discounted sales price, perhaps on offer via an auction house? Such properties may or may not be repossessed. Often auction properties may be in excellent condition and not require any renovation, enabling you to sell on at a profit immediately.
- Have a location in an increasingly popular area, but not an overpriced, 'high-end' location? Perhaps there is a lot of other new residential developments, retail outlets, a bustling high street, good transport and other amenities.
- Have structural problems? Such properties are troublesome, if not impossible, to buy with a mortgage. If you are a cash buyer, though, you can purchase such a building at a greatly discounted price if you are prepared to undertake substantial repairs before re-selling.
- Have period/character features? In the UK, period properties tend to hold their value quite well. They are usually the first to increase in value when a 'downmarket' area becomes fashionable. It is also important to bear in mind, when renovating a period property, the importance of maintaining character. For example, it can deter buyers of

a Victorian property if it has been renovated with modern-style doors, windows, banisters, etc.

## GETTING READY TO SELL

While planning your development schedule for any given property, it is important to bear in mind a timeline and procedures for putting it back on the market.

- Choose your 'For Sale' date. When will the property be ready to put on the market? Will it be a good time of year? If not, plan renovations accordingly. Refer to chapter 4 regarding timing.
- Choose your marketing method. Consult two or three estate agents to realistically value your property. For the quickest sale, hire an agent to market it for you and guide you through the negotiation process with potential buyers to achieve the best price possible. Bear in mind you will have to pay a sales commission which can be up to 2%.
- You could sell the property without an agent and market it yourself via property websites. However, as an overseas vendor that may

prove rather time-consuming and complicated without, at least, a representative in the UK to arrange viewings for prospective buyers. Alternatively, you could instruct Timo Real Estate Solutions whose staff have got vast experience and broad knowledge of the UK property market. They are certainly in a better position to find the most suitable property investment at a discounted rate for you.

- Once ready to go on the market, make an effort to 'stage' your property to help achieve the best prices. This includes not only full decoration in terms of painting and cleaning, gardening, but also displaying light furnishing to show how the property might function as a home (furniture and interior décor rental outlets can assist here). Some prospective buyers simply can't visualise their potential new home in an empty flat or house.

## GROWING YOUR UK PROPERTY PORTFOLIO

Following on from the chapter on Wealth Diversification, in my opinion, the most important strategy for success as a property investor is to build a portfolio of properties that aims to achieve BOTH rental and capital growth, for both the short and long term. For the more adventurous investor, turn to the chapter on land development.

- Firstly, consider why you want to invest in UK property, rather than, for example, stocks and shares, for your financial goals. Do you prefer the 'safety' of investing in long-term 'bricks and mortar'? Why the UK? Is it a dream of yours to own a London apartment or English country cottage?
- Do your research about the property market in the UK and choose a location.
- Learn about property types which interest you most and location 'hotspots'.
- Shop around for the best mortgage products. Keep on track of your accounts and financial situation, particularly when forecasting rental income against mortgage costs. Seek professional advice whenever possible.
- Learn about financing/mortgage options in the UK. Opt for freehold properties when possible, for the sake of simplicity during conveyancing if nothing else. The main advantage of buying property on a freehold tenure is that he or she owns it outright, including the land on which it is built.

- For rental properties, envisage your ideal tenant and consider your management responsibilities. As an overseas investor, you will need a management agent to look after this for you. Don't forget to factor in fees for rental management.

## Breaking Barriers

The property investment industry has been a staple of the global economy for centuries. It is indeed an avenue via which shrewd decision-making can prove greatly rewarding both financially and personally. Successful property tycoons dominate the popular 'rich lists' of the world with regularity. Property has been, and always will be, a worthwhile and attractive means of investing your money, time and effort.

However, you may still be reluctant to dip your toe in the property pond. If so, ask yourself why? I am of the opinion that, given the proper tools and knowledge, anyone can become a property investor and achieve their desired wealth and goals. In this section I hope to help you remove any obstacles or excuses preventing you from embarking on your property investment dreams.

As an overseas investor, this reluctance may be greater. If you are a novice, start small, perhaps with a low-risk buy-to-let option. If you are a seasoned investor in your own country but are looking for a new challenge, the UK offers endless opportunities. If your own country has an unstable economy, the UK is likely a much safer bet for your money.

Whether you have purchased this book purely for the sake of general knowledge and interest, or you are determined to achieve investment 'gold' in the UK, you have taken the first step to becoming a UK property investor, should you so wish.

Property investment, like any other business, must be run professionally and efficiently to succeed. It is essentially a logical process, but one that also requires creative and sensible strategies to reap great financial reward.

To get your property business up and running, one needs to be mindful of the following potential obstacles and prepare to overcome them:

- Not having sufficient capital to get started
- Inadequate knowledge and experience to make informed, strategic decisions

- Poor credit history preventing you from obtaining easy access to bank financing
- Lacking in personal drive; are you ambitious but don't quite have the drive to see through a development project on your own?
- Afraid of risk
- Not prepared financially for the unexpected; could you deal with tenants not paying rent one month? What about absentee builders in the middle of a renovation? What if the variable interest rate rose dramatically?

All the above can be overcome! Timo Real Estate Solutions can advise on contingency plans and guide you in resolving such issues. Let's find out how.

## FINANCE

Of course, the biggest obstacle when starting any business venture is raising enough capital to get things off the ground. Unless you have saved a great deal or inherited a tidy sum, chances are you will be applying for a mortgage on your first property. Whether you are buying your first home or your first investment property, a deposit must be paid with any mortgage.

As an overseas investor, you will be aware of, and were probably affected by, the last economic recession that hit countries worldwide. The UK was not spared, by any means, and hence banks here have tightened considerably their requirements for approving mortgage applications. Among other demands, these days, banks often want greater details regarding employment history, require proof of address over longer periods, and are increasingly fussy over poor credit history and as such require larger deposits than previously. The bottom line is, obtaining a mortgage in the UK is not as easy as it once was. Having said that, it is not impossible by any means! In fact, these stricter eligibility requirements do have an upside for the investor. With fewer mortgage applications being approved, there may be fewer competitors on the property ladder, meaning more properties are available, thus creating a 'buyer's market' in some areas. You could end up buying your ideal property at a discounted rate.

There are several options available to you for raising funding for your property project, other than a new mortgage or loan. These may include:

- Use a combination of personal savings, investments, inheritance, family gifting.

- Re-mortgage other properties, if applicable. Even if you don't need to access funds, do keep an eye on the interest rates of your other mortgage(s) as it may be prudent to switch lenders.
- Acquire a cash-rich investment partner; this could be a passive 'silent' partner, who wishes only to lend the money for a good return in a given period of time, or it could be a more vocal partner with whom you can share the entire investment/development project and truly 'be in it together'.
- Earn funds from another sideline business or employment opportunity; this is essentially saving from scratch and may take you a while, but the property business isn't going anywhere and it will wait for you! The upside here is, you won't have any ties to a partner or need to pay out any interest on a loan.
- Upon completion of your first development and sale, or after collecting rental income for an extended period of time, put a good percentage of your profits back into your business for the next venture. Then take the next step into building your property portfolio. It is good practice to do this regularly, varying

the percentage as you see fit, with the completion of each and every project until you reach your portfolio goals and beyond.

But first things first – obtaining that first lump sum of capital as either the deposit or renovation fund to get the ball rolling. Naturally, these steps are also applicable to the experienced investors who find themselves in a cash-poor situation. Consider the following logical steps:

1. Write down all your possible and practical sources of financing from the suggestions above.
2. Pick the three most suitable and plan a proposal strategy. There will likely be a different approach required for different sources, whether they be a family member or a bank – in any case, each one warrants a thoroughly professional and prepared meeting.
3. Draft a comprehensive and detailed property investment proposal, stating:
    a. How you intend to build and manage your portfolio over the next 10 years

b. How you intend to pay back the lender's money that you have borrowed

## KNOWLEDGE

Lack of knowledge in any business is a recipe for failure, to be sure. The beauty of property investment is that anyone, regardless of education or experience, can gain the knowledge required to succeed in property development – if they have the drive. With the online world at our fingertips, it is possible to simply read about everything you need to know – starting with this book, of course! I sincerely hope you find my content useful for expanding your knowledge. It is vital to acquire as much information as possible before any new property venture, particularly as an overseas developer investing in a country that is not your home. The phrase "knowledge is power" has never been more apt.

Where other industries require degrees and internships, all one needs to embark on a property development career is common sense, the tenacity to read up on the specifics of the industry, as well as a deep-rooted ambition to succeed.

If you identify what is needed to achieve your property investment goals, there is no reason why you can't raise the necessary funds to make it happen. It may take some time to fund your first project, but once you get started it is entirely realistic to anticipate completing one buy-to-sell property per year.

Later in the book you will find some handy additional resources to foster your increasing knowledge. Check out the glossary to explain the common British property and financing jargon that you may find confusing, particularly if English is not your first language. A selection of useful links will help you to discover more about virtually any given property-related topic.

## CREDIT HISTORY

Part of the financing approval process with a bank or other lending company involves a credit check. In the UK, most lenders will commonly use the credit reporting agencies Experian and Equifax to review your credit history before offering a mortgage or loan.

It is therefore extremely important to keep your credit reputation clean – stay on top of any credit card payments and utility bills. The more attractive your credit history, the more likely you are to be granted loans with more favourable terms and lower interest rates.

If you do have a less-than-perfect credit history, do not despair. There are lenders who specialise only in the sub-prime market; bear in mind they normally charge higher rates.

For foreign property investors, however, this may not be applicable; there are UK lenders who do grant loans specifically to overseas-based clients. Timo Real Estate Solutions not only will help you obtain the property you desire, but can also help you source the best financing package to suit your requirements.

For UK residents, you can learn about your own credit history via credit checker websites such as www.experian.co.uk and www.equifax.co.uk.

You will find helpful tips to improve your UK credit rating in the *Additional Resources* chapter at the end of the book.

## ATTITUDE

There is no doubt that property investment projects demand a lot of hard work and focus. If you possess a positive attitude and the drive to get ahead, you will be in good stead to make informed, strategic decisions for successful investments. If you have, shall we say, "casual work ethics" and/or lack confidence, those are personal obstacles that can be overcome in time. I do sincerely hope this book motivates you to grow in enthusiasm, drive and confidence to venture forth with your property investment dreams!

## THE ECONOMIC CLIMATE

One obstacle to overcome that is out of our control when it comes to property investment is the state of the economic climate. Regardless of your country, whether it is the UK, Dubai or Nigeria, once a recession or depression hits your business could suffer greatly, no matter how well you've been managing your portfolio. You may find, for instance, your rental tenants have suffered redundancy and are unable to pay the rent. You may find it difficult to re-mortgage one of your properties as lenders have restricted approval criteria in a time of economic downturn. During periods of economic uncertainty, proceed cautiously in your ventures and maintain relevant insurance policies to protect yourself, your family and your business.

* * * * * * * * *

At the heart of the issue, of course, is money. In earlier chapters, we've detailed the various ways to finance your venture – so we know that problem can be solved. You may be doubtful of your knowledge, experience and courage to see it through. With the guidance and encouragement of Timo Real Estate Solutions – we know those doubts can be relieved.

There is a lot to consider when starting your property portfolio. It is a lot of work, no doubt! The key to success is in identifying what your goals really are. Form your strategy, with budget and schedule in mind, and you are set to go!

Timo Real Estate Solutions can hold your hand and guide you every step of the way!

* * * * * * * * *

Coming up, we will review the basics of property law. While you will have a solicitor working on your behalf to deal with property conveyancing, it is helpful to gain some understanding in advance of what you may be required to pay in terms of government taxes.

# Chapter 11
# Property Law & Conveyancing

## Tax basics and conveyancing stages

Regardless of your country of residence, government taxes are an unavoidable consequence of property investment. For both domestic and overseas investors, it is prudent to familiarise yourself with the basics of UK property law and which taxes you can expect to be paying. There is varying legislation in the UK regarding property charges, with tax costs dependent on both the value of the property and the buyer's circumstance. This chapter will help to demystify what is required of investors in terms of property law with facts sourced from the UK government website, www.gov.uk, which I recommend you refer to in future for the very latest information.

**VALUE ADDED TAX (VAT)**

If you are planning to invest in any type of commercial property, bear in mind that the government applies VAT to all commercial property transactions. That means 20% of the property's value will be charged! That can add up to a hefty amount even on small development projects. Value Added Tax is NOT, however, charged on any residential properties, including buy-to-let. If you are looking to save money on tax expenses, if you are on a very tight budget, then residential would be the way to go.

## STAMP DUTY

In England, Wales and Northern Ireland, all categories of property, both residential and commercial, are subject to Stamp Duty Land Tax (SDLT). Stamp Duty no longer applies in Scotland where, instead, you pay Land and Buildings Transaction Tax when purchasing property. The SDLT percentage charged varies according to the property's intended use, such as whether it will be a mixed-use (both residential and commercial) development or earn substantial rent.

According to www.gov.uk, as of December 2017, the starting thresholds for paying SDLT as of $1^{st}$ July 2017 are as follows:

- £125,000 for residential properties
- £150,000 for non-residential land and properties

The tax is calculated on increasing portions of the property price above these thresholds, starting at 2%. Thresholds for freehold and leasehold residential, at the time of writing, are:

| | |
|---|---|
| *Up to £125,000* | *0%* |
| *The next £125,000 (the portion from £125,001 - £250,000)* | *2%* |
| *The next £675,000 (the portion from £250,001 - £925,000)* | *5%* |
| *The next £575,000 (the portion from £975,000 - £1.5 million)* | *10%* |
| *The remaining amount (the portion above £1.5 million)* | *12%* |

There is great news if you are a first-time buyer – you are entitled to the following discounts when purchasing a property up to £500,000:

- Up to £300,000 purchase price – 0% SDLT
- Between £300,000 and £500,000 – 5% SDLT (due on that portion of the price only)

As an investor, you can see the benefit of making sure your purchase price is below the next threshold. Paying one penny more over £925,000 means you'll have pay 10% tax on the relevant portion rather than 5%.

For other property types and special circumstances, there are various exceptions and other considerations regarding SDLT, for instance in cases of commercial property, multiple-property purchases, mixed-use, shared ownership situations, and therefore I recommend you refer to www.gov.uk for further details. You will also find there a handy SDLT calculator for determining the amount payable for both residential and non-residential, freehold and leasehold properties.

**INCOME TAX**

UK-resident investors in the UK property market need to take into account the issue of income tax. Any profit you make on a property investment is, indeed, considered an income in the UK and as such is subject to income tax. There is a personal allowance which is not taxable; any amount over that limit is taxed at a percentage rate depending on the amount of profit/earnings. Investors not resident in the UK are not typically subject to income tax, however there are instances whereby a foreign investor could be charged upwards of 20% on profits from buy-to-let properties, depending on the profit margin.

Personal allowance and tax rates can vary year upon year and so should be checked via www.gov.uk or with your financial advisor or solicitor.

## CAPITAL GAINS TAX

Property investors must pay capital gains tax when selling or giving away a property that is not their main residence, such as a buy-to-let or investment property, or second home or business premises. Overseas investors are not subject to this tax. There are exceptions to this rule though, so it is prudent to ensure your solicitor or financial advisor guides you accordingly.

## NON-RESIDENT LANDLORD SCHEME

UK property landlords must comply with the Non-Resident Landlord Scheme if they are resident overseas for more than six months of the year. The tax is typically administered through the tenant or letting agent, who deducts the tax amount from the rent owing to the landlord. There are certain exemptions though so do take advice on this prior to embarking on a buy-to-let project.

For most overseas investors, entering the UK property arena can be very lucrative with few restrictions. In terms of property law, knowledge of which taxes, if any, you are required to pay will put you in good stead for budgeting and profit forecasting of your portfolio.

## LAND REGISTRY

The government's Land Registry department keeps a record of all property ownership and must be notified of every property purchase. Such information is held as public record, including all previous owners and the relevant sales prices, whether it was freehold or leasehold and if any changes have been made to the property or plot.

## THE CONVEYANCING PROCESS

The entire conveyancing process for handling your property transactions will be undertaken by a solicitor of your choosing. Being aware of conveyancing steps and stages is helpful to understand and gauge how long the process may take and what obstacles may crop up along the way. The stages below are typical, but not exhaustive, of an uncomplicated purchase property in the UK.

## Conveyancing for Buying a Property

1. The buyer makes an offer on a property, which is accepted by the seller, and instructs a solicitor to handle the conveyancing.
2. The buyer instigates a property survey to take place and applies (if applicable) for a mortgage.
3. The seller's solicitor will supply a Contract Pack. The contract of sale and supporting documents will be reviewed; queries will be raised and discussed/resolved with the seller's solicitor. The buyer's solicitor also undertakes any necessary searches and obtains a copy of the mortgage offer, if applicable.
4. The buyer's solicitor prepares a detailed Contract Report which the buyer reviews. Any queries will be raised and dealt with. When the buyer is happy to proceed, the deposit sum is paid to the buyer's solicitor in preparation for the exchange of contracts.
5. The buyer and seller agree on a completion date and contracts are formally 'exchanged' – meaning both parties are legally committed to the transaction from that point onwards.

6. The buyer's solicitor prepares a draft transfer deed and completion information form, which the seller's solicitor approves and a final copy is made.
7. The buyer's seller prepares a completion statement, carries out any remaining searches and applies to the buyer's mortgage lender for the mortgage loan.
8. On completion day, the seller vacates the property by the agreed time and the buyer's solicitor sends the proceeds of sale to the seller's solicitor. The seller's solicitor then releases the keys to the estate agent or buyer directly and sends the title deeds and transfer deed to the buyer's solicitor and ensures the repayment of any existing mortgage on the property.
9. The buyer's solicitor sends the stamp duty payable to HMRC, receives the title deeds, transfer deed and proof that the seller has paid the outstanding mortgage on the property.
10. The buyer's solicitor registers the property in the name of the buyer at the Land Registry and a copy is sent to the buyer and the mortgage lender (if applicable).

\* \* \* \* \* \* \* \* \* \*

In chapter 12, I would like to talk about the importance of obtaining independent advice and explore further opportunities (yes, there are more!) for developing your property business, including the benefits of setting up a formal property investment company and joining forces with an investment syndicate.

# Chapter 12
# Further Considerations

*Independent advice, company registration, property investment syndicates*

It is worth saying, once again, that all you truly need to start a property investment business is common sense, courage and determination. In tangible terms, of course, a level of deposit and renovation funding is needed also but without the drive to obtain the money in the first place, you won't get out of the starting blocks. In this chapter, we will discuss the importance of obtaining independent advice, recap financing essentials, advise the benefits of setting up a company and explore property syndicates.

**OBTAINING INDEPENDENT ADVICE**

As discussed, the most common source of obtaining financing for your first property is via a mortgage. In the United Kingdom, there are currently more than 80 mortgage providers listed in the Council of Mortgage Lenders Directory. That is quite an overwhelming list to choose from when looking for a mortgage product that best suits your circumstances. If you already have an account with a UK bank or building society, you would, understandably, be tempted to simply approach the staff mortgage advisor for guidance on your budding property portfolio dreams without shopping around elsewhere. This may well be the most straightforward route – if you meet your bank's lending criteria your application will be approved and you can proceed without delay.

However, the disadvantage with seeking a mortgage only with your local bank or building society is that, while you and the lender know and trust one another, they may not be able to offer you the best mortgage product on the market. Your bank can offer only their products. As a result, you may end up making higher payments than necessary and be tied into terms that aren't ideal for you and your scheduling plans.

This is where the services of an independent mortgage advisor or broker come in handy! A good independent advisor is very knowledgeable about the broad UK mortgage industry and is well qualified to assist you in obtaining the most suitable mortgage for your circumstances and requirements. Even if you consider yourself well-read and informed regarding general issues of property finance, the professionals are on top of the ever-changing details within the mortgage market on any given day.

As in any service industry, it is good practice to seek a mortgage advisor based on reputation and personal recommendation. Good references, based on actual personal experience, are crucial. Your mortgage advisor will be privy to all your personal details and finances – you must join forces with someone you trust and respect implicitly.

As an overseas investor, you may have friends in the UK who can recommend an advisor. If not, Timo Real Estate Solutions has a number of clients who are happy to provide a testimonial.

An independent mortgage advisor will be able to find you the most appropriate mortgage product from the entire pool of UK lenders. Advisors are particularly useful when it comes to finding the best deals for very large mortgage sums and unusual properties – an advisor can even help to source and arrange a tailor-made mortgage rather than simply offering what is advertised on the high street.

Some advisors charge a fee, others do not. Those who do not charge generally earn a commission from whichever lender they have secured a mortgage with on behalf of their client. Such commission varies. I am sure you can see how this may be open to preferential treatment between an advisor and lender. This is not to say your advisor would probably be swayed by larger commissions rather than your best interest, but it is a possibility to bear in mind if you do not already have a trusted relationship with your advisor.

Most independent mortgage advisors charge a fee. This, in my opinion, is a testament of commitment and motivation; independents charging a fee must work hard to prove their worth to clients.

In any case, it is prudent to research your options regardless of whether you are applying to only one lender directly or seeking independent advice. It could make a significant difference to your monthly cash outlay and commitments.

**RECAPPING MORTGAGE OPTIONS**

As discussed at length in the earlier chapters on financing and mortgages, it is worth recapping the factors to consider when choosing a mortgage product. Do you want the peace of mind that comes with stable monthly payments? Or do you want the lowest payments possible and plan to redeem the mortgage in the short term if you are planning a quick flip project? Weigh up all the fees on the table before choosing, including redemption penalties and insurance. Your mortgage advisor will be of great service in helping make this decision. Method of repayment: interest-only, standard repayment or a combination of the two.

a) Length of mortgage term: the longer the term, the smaller the monthly repayments; the shorter the term, less interest is due. Standard terms in the UK are usually 25 years but it is possible to extend this to 30.

b) Type of interest rate: choose from fixed, variable, discounted, capped, among others. Bear in mind the likely interest rate that will apply once your agreed period comes to an end.

c) Lender's charges: these vary and can include mortgage administration (set up) fees, valuation fees, Mortgage Indemnity Guarantee (MIG) costs, or a High Percentage Lending Fee (HPLF) if you are putting down a very small deposit.

## RECAPPING OPTIONS TO RAISE A DEPOSIT

If you haven't got savings or a 'gift' to speak of, your options for raising a deposit for an investment property mortgage are:

a) Increase the mortgage on your current home, if applicable. This is a straightforward, simple option.
b) Increase the mortgage on another property in your portfolio.
c) Personal or business loan.
d) Credit card advance or bank overdraft extension.[*]

Methods a) and b) are ideal if the new property you are seeking is in such poor condition that a lender would not approve a mortgage on it. The goal when it comes to financing new properties is to plan ahead carefully with minimal risk and obtain the most cost-effective lending, whether it be for a single project or multiple.

---

[*] I recommend this only if you are an experienced property investor and confident of a quick flip scenario – it is not the ideal option and is very risky indeed.

## SETTING UP A PROPERTY INVESTMENT COMPANY

Investments carried out through a company status or other commercial vehicle project an air of professionalism, encouraging you to run your business in an organised fashion that will prove beneficial when it comes to raising funds. In the UK, the most popular business registrations are: Sole Trader, Partnership or a Limited company. Establishing business status is not restricted to residents, overseas investors are fully able to set up UK-based businesses.

Running your property investments through a registered business, separately from your personal life and financing, will enable you to maintain organised, easy to access files and office systems. A company name also comes across to lenders and other business associates as professional and in time, reliable and reputable. Let's look more closely at the differences between the most comment business setups:

### Sole trader

In this case, you have full control over the business and a sole right to claim any and all profits your company generates. It is a straightforward process to set up as a sole trader and not expensive. The only downside to sole trader status is that you are fully personally responsible and liable for the business. As your property portfolio grows, so does this responsibility. There is no legal protection from debts or claims for a sole trader. You will be exposed to unlimited liability if any debts accrue.

**Partnership**

You may prefer to work together with like-minded colleagues in your property investment business, in which case setting up an official partnership is a good option. A registered partnership may have up to 20 individuals trading together. You and your partnerships can combine capital, skills and time to devote to the execution of your property developments and projects. Each person is equal in the partnership, in all aspects of running the business. So, too, is each person equally responsible for any business debts and issues that occur. Furthermore, each partner is also responsible for the debts another partner, regardless of their knowledge of it. This scenario can be avoided, though, with the arrangement of a limited partnership. With a limited partnership, it is made clear to all parties the details of individual contributions and responsibilities. A reputable solicitor can raise a 'Deed of Partnership' which, albeit not required by law, can prove very useful in times of difficulty or dispute.

## Limited company

A limited company is a legal entity in its own right. The main advantage of a limited company (particularly a private limited liability company) is that the liability of the company owners/shareholders for any losses the company might make are literally limited, normally to a nominal amount. In small companies, the directors are often employees as well as being in charge of day-to-day business. Registering your business as a limited company is also a good way of attracting other investors. Some property entrepreneurs set up multiple limited companies whereby each investor owns part of the portfolio and outside investors can be brought in to collaborate on different projects. This 'beehive' system affords a greater degree of limited liability protection − if one company fails, the others can proceed unaffected. There are often corporation tax advantages with a limited company too, particularly when starting your first business − small limited companies pay a lower rate of corporation tax than a sole trader business of a similar size.

Are there disadvantages? Yes. The accounting responsibilities required for this type of business are substantial! In the UK, the accounts must be prepared by a qualified accountant on an annual basis and filed with Companies House. Additionally, as a limited company benefits from *unlimited* liability, you may need to personally guarantee any mortgages or other form of credit (which does, in fact, reduce the benefit of limited liability somewhat).

## PROPERTY INVESTMENT SYNDICATE (PIS)

Similar to a partnership company, a Property Investment Syndicate, or PIS, is a collective of people investing in properties together – pooling resources and skills – striving to make great profit through development. Syndicate members may be of the silent variety, contributing only money, not time and effort, or they may both invest and work on executing the projects. The primary advantage of a PIS is that it allows you to raise a large amount of capital and undertake big, complex and ultimately more profitable projects from the start. You don't need to build up investment capital gradually, with smaller projects, as you do when developing on your own. The only disadvantage is that you must share profits and control of the business with all members.

Your syndicate could be made up of friends and family, spreading the outlay and risk with people you already have a relationship with. If you don't know of anyone with sufficient funds or the desire to form a syndicate with you, make enquiries with estate agents, or your bank manager, who will probably know of private investors who are open to syndicates. Try your solicitor and accountant as well for private investor contacts. Timo Real Estate Solutions, too, are able to assist in the introduction to a syndicate.

### Setting up a Property Investment Syndicate

Setting up a syndicate is a great way of getting started in property development, especially if you have little or no money at all to invest. The strategy with a PIS, like any development, is to work hard to get the project started, manage it professionally and complete on time and within budget, spreading the profit amongst syndicate members upon completion.

The beauty of a PIS is that the structure is dictated by the members. There is no official structure required legally. It would be prudent, though, to have a solicitor draw up a comprehensive contract outlining the members' agreement.

There is no minimum or maximum number of syndicate members, although a common range is somewhere between five and 20. Contributing factors include the duration of the project, level of investment and anticipated returns. Shares are allocated according to the percentage of cash investment from each member.

Each member must be made fully aware of all details regarding the financial risk involved; like any investment, investors may or may not make a good profit and, worst-case scenario, they could lose money.

Syndicate members are not necessarily owners of the property being developed. The property deeds would normally be held in your name or the name of the company.

If the syndicate members decide they wish to invest in the ownership of the property in question, there are two options: form a limited liability company as discussed previously or form a legal co-operative, which is more suitable if members prefer to be directly involved throughout the development.

Once you have received all members' investment payments, you may proceed with your project(s). It is advisable to keep members well informed about progress, from new purchases to refurbishment plans and costings. Such updates must also be done upon the completion of each project and at the end of the relevant financial year, with prepared accounts indicating all expenses, total income and net profit generated. It is this profit that will then be distributed accordingly, based on the investment share of each member.

With a nice tidy profit from your share of the PIS tucked in the bank, you can now use those funds to start up another, bigger syndicate, investing more of your own money in a new development, hopefully increasing profits with each new project. Following this method over a few years, you will eventually accrue sufficient funds to bankroll a development entirely on your own.

* * * * * * * * *

Now that we have learned about setting up a company in the UK and how Property Investment Syndicates work, I'd like to share with you more of my personal journey which hopefully may inspire you in one way or another!

# Chapter 13
# My Personal Journey

*Pursuing the dream*

For those of you who have not read my first book, *Property Investment: Create Your Own Legacy*, I would like to share with you the story of my journey from my home country of Uganda in March 1997 to my life now in the UK as a successful Property and Mortgage Consultant. It may be that you can draw some comparisons to your own life and gain inspiration from my story and thoughts, with increased motivation to achieve your own goals in life. If indeed you have read my first book, please allow me this opportunity to share once again!

I am really glad that my parents did their very best to create a warm home environment of which I have very fond memories. On the other hand, there was a lot of insecurity when I was growing up. It usually felt very unsafe whenever I stepped out of our home to go to school. As you can imagine, a lot of people lost their lives. I am very glad and so grateful indeed that I am still here, alive and kicking!

During those dark days, especially in my teenage years, that's when I would dream about moving to no other country but the United Kingdom and London, the great city in particular, just to see what it had to offer and also for self-development. It was a dream that I had in mind and worked so hard to achieve for about 10 years. I feel that I could easily write another book about this specific subject, not only for the sake of patting my own back but maybe to inspire anyone out there that, despite any odds or obstacles, you can achieve your dreams too! In my humble opinion, all it takes is the vision, the plan of action and the sheer will or determination to pursue it.

I must admit settling in the UK was the hardest thing I have ever done in my entire life! Initially, I was naive to think that coming to London would be so easy and straightforward. Little did I know that I had to find my own shelter over my head and something to eat to stay alive! Worse still, the pace of lifestyle was much faster than what I was used to and I hardly knew anyone here for support! Ironically, I didn't feel any cultural shock as so many others do, but other aspects like different transport systems, shopping habits, food tastes, to mention but a few, certainly gave me a reality check! I had to change my mind-set quickly to adapt to my new environment. In hindsight, I could have done a lot of things differently if I knew then what I know now. Basically, the first five years of my life in the UK were hell and I wouldn't wish my personal experience on anyone else. However, in terms of character building, I am a lot stronger and wiser for it. For this reason, I feel so blessed and very proud that not only do I live in London, the greatest city on the planet, but I've managed also to work so hard and place myself in such a position that I can share my experiences and knowledge with you. If my personal journey and the information contained in this book makes a significant positive difference in the life of anyone reading any of my books, I would be the happiest man in the world!

In fact, my main priority and biggest challenge that I have set for myself, for the next five years (from 1st January 2018 to 31$^{st}$ December 2022) is to touch and improve the lives of 1,000,000 people (YES, I said it... One MILLION). Ask me HOW?

Please do not hesitate to visit my website, www.timoseks.com, where I shall be updating you about the progress of my enormous but achievable challenge and if you don't mind, please share those posts or blogs about this initiative to your friends and family members.

In the meantime, now that I have found my calling in life and am achieving my dream of financial freedom, I would like to inspire others in my home country and beyond to reap the opportunities and rewards that property investment in the UK can bring.

When I started out in the property business I was making a decent living but, at one point, I lost virtually everything. It was during the recession here in the UK in 2008 when things fell apart. Once again, it was a bitter lesson learned. Be brave and take calculated risks only.

I therefore had to go back to the drawing board, live within my means and start afresh. Right now, I am very positive about what the future holds not only for me and my family but for all those people out there in the world whose lives I am going to work so hard for, to touch and improve. I simply can't wait!!!

The fact that I was able to build my business from nothing, a second time, is a story I am incredibly proud of and want to share with others. With this, my second book, I am reaching out in particular to potential investors outside the UK – those whom I know have great admiration for the United Kingdom, truly a land of opportunity. I want to teach others not only about the ins and outs of the real estate industry in the UK, but how to avoid the early mistakes I made. Most importantly, I want to share the fact that ANYONE, armed with the right knowledge, can make great financial gain through property investment in the UK – even though you reside in another country!

As we have discussed, streams of property income are so varied: rent properties for passive income, residentially or commercially; acquire equity through re-mortgage; renovate and sell quickly for short-term income or sell and hold on for long-term capital growth; asset stripping; land development – all of which and more have been covered in this book.

Three years ago, I announced my intention to achieve my ambitious personal goals of attaining absolute financial freedom within five years.

However you decide to start investing in property, whether your ambition is to have one beautiful apartment in central London (that you can rent out but also use for your own family holidays) or if your aim is to have a wide-ranging commercial property portfolio, I have written this book to provide you with the tools and inspiration to do so. Rest assured you are now armed with enough knowledge to embark upon your property business.

There is absolutely no reason why you can't achieve the success you desire through shrewd property investments. What is the difference between you and the multi-multimillionaire tycoons we read about? Nothing – except they actually took the first step to make it happen. Your first step... go to *Chapter 3: Entering the Arena.*

As I've mentioned previously, becoming a property investor requires courage, and that requires strength of character. Being an independent entrepreneur involves a lot of 'weight on one's shoulders' at times. Let me indulge myself for a moment and offer you, in my humble opinion, my thoughts on the skills and traits that one can work on to foster the strength of character needed to pursue those big investment dreams:

1. Identify who you are and what you want to achieve in life. What are your strengths and weaknesses? What do you want to achieve in

life, both personally and professionally? Answering these questions will help you formulate a sense of direction and purpose to succeed.
2. Make good, positive choices in lifestyle, relationships (both personally and professionally), career; think about what you want in the future.
3. The old adage: "It's not just what you know, it's also who you know." Maintaining good relationships and networking are key in the property world, whether it be with estate agents making you a priority for discounted properties, or solicitors who put your conveyancing to the top of the work pile and do their utmost to stop a deal from falling through!
4. Be a good listener; you never know what you may learn!

Thank you for entertaining my personal story on the road to real estate success! As we near the end of this book, I hope you will find the following Additional Resources to be useful information tools.

# Chapter 14
# Additional Resources

This chapter collates a selection of resources you can refer to as and when needed.

## *The Planning Permission Process*

Property and land development permission must be obtained from the relevant local council authority. The application process, generally, may be summarised in six key stages. The procedure is largely governed according to council legislation and is designed to incorporate feedback of experts and all parties concerned in the decision-making process. Prior to making a formal application, it is recommended that you contact a planning officer for proposal advice, which may highlight any issues that could delay your application.

### Step 1 – Application registration
Submit your completed application form (either online or hard copy by post). Detailed guidance can be found on the council's website, where you can download all relevant forms. Upon receipt by the

council, the application is checked and registered. Any missing information is requested.

### Step 2 – Consultation and publicity
The planning proposal is sent to various expert parties for consultation. Advertisements, where required, are placed in the appropriate local media for the public's information, advising how one can view proposed plans and post comments, usually 21 days from the date of publishing.

### Step 3 – Consideration
The assigned planning case officer inspects the site, considering planning policy, consultation responses and public feedback received.

### Step 4 – Negotiation
If the planning officer identifies resolvable issues with the application, the applicant is requested to make such amendments. It may then be necessary to repeat steps 2 and 3 if the changes are significant.

### Step 5 – Recommendation
The planning officer makes a recommendation to the relevant authority for a decision to be made, either by the Director of Planning or by elected members at an area committee meeting. Most applications are decided by the Director of Planning. Committee

meeting decisions are made at a public event whereby the time and venue are advised in advance and interested parties may voice their objections.

## Step 6 – Decision
The relevant body takes a decision on the application and issues a decision notice to the applicant or agent.

## Tips to Improve Your Credit Rating

Take the following steps to help improve your credit rating. Also bear in mind certain behaviours to minimise that are considered a sign of poor money management by lenders, such as withdrawing cash on credit cards and taking payday loans. Stability is a plus – living at the same address, being employed in the same job (with the same employer) and having the same bank account for a reasonable period of time will be a help in achieving and maintaining a good credit record.

For an overseas investor, who does not reside in the UK, you will not have a credit rating here – good or bad. However, this will not hinder you when it comes to obtaining a mortgage or commercial finance from a UK lender as they will do their own due diligence and check on potential buyers prior to approving any loans.

1. **Check your credit report**

    Before you apply for any type of loan, check your credit report for accuracy with a credit reference agency such as www.experian.co.uk. Ensure your credit record shows correct address details. You can view this on a free trial basis or by paying a small fee. Check your report annually or before any major loan application. There may be errors that need to be rectified. Check again if your application is rejected.

2. **Get on the electoral register**

   This will improve your chances of being accepted for credit. Prospective lenders and credit reference agencies use the electoral register to prove your identity and residency are accurate.

3. **Pay off any outstanding debts**

   Where possible, pay off in full any outstanding debt, with more than just the minimum monthly payments. This an indication of responsible money management to lenders.

4. **Sever financial ties**

   A partner's personal credit history can affect yours if you share any bank accounts or loans. When you and your spouse/partner obtain a joint mortgage or joint bank account, the pair of you become financially linked. It also prudent to inform the credit reference agencies of your disassociation if you and your spouse/partner separate or divorce and therefore, you no longer share a financial product.

5. **Cancel unused cards and direct debits**

    Close any old and no longer used credit card accounts, store cards and direct debits. Lenders may consider the amount of credit you have access to, as well as the amount of debt you owe. Cutting up cards is not enough – you need to physically contact the provider and close the account!

6. **Get a new credit card**

    Rebuild your credit history with a new credit card. If you've never had credit before, it's difficult for a lender to assess you. Make a couple of purchases on it each month and repay the balance in full by the due date with a direct debit. This will show that you can responsibly manage credit.

7. **Pay your bills on time**

    Never be late or miss a payment, whether it be for the electricity or a mobile phone bill. Missed and late payments can stay on your credit file for up to six years. If you've made a late payment due to circumstances beyond your control (i.e. your direct debit wasn't set up in time), so long as you made the payment promptly when you noticed, talk to your credit provider and see if you can get this black mark removed.

8. **Apply for a prepaid credit card**

   A prepaid credit card can quickly help you improve your rating. For a monthly fee (about £5), which you'll need to keep paying for 12 months, you will acquire an entry to your credit file stating that you have successfully repaid a debt. A prepaid card doesn't require a credit reference as you don't borrow on it.

9. **Consider timing**

   Don't apply for several loans too close together. If you have old issues that are due to expire shortly (e.g. court judgments), wait until such time has passed.

10. **Minimise your credit applications**

    Credit reference agencies are not informed if you are rejected for credit, but a note is made every time a lender undertakes a credit search. The more credit searches in your name are carried out in a short space of time, the less likely you are to be approved for credit. Therefore, it makes sense to space out your credit applications and, if possible, find out whether you're likely to be accepted before applying – you can do this via free eligibility calculators online.

## Top 10 UK Auction Houses for Property

*(in alphabetical order)*

1. Allsop
   Considered by many as the leading UK property auctioneer with offices in London, Leeds and Brighton. They hold several residential and commercial auctions throughout the year.
   www.allsop.co.uk

2. Auction House
   The UK's largest residential property auction company, with several locations throughout England, Wales and Scotland.
   www.auctionhouse.co.uk

3. Barnard Marcus:
   Represents properties throughout the UK; auctions are held in central London.
   www.barnardmarcusauctions.co.uk

4. Barnett Ross

    A leading independent firm specialising in the sale of both commercial property nationwide and residential property in London, Middlesex and Hertfordshire.

    www.barnettross.co.uk

5. Brown & Co

    A growing auctioneer with offices throughout East Anglia, the Midlands and Yorkshire, specialising in rural property.

    www.brown-co.com

6. Countrywide

    Auctioning residential, commercial, industrial, agricultural properties and land across the UK with 24 auctions annually.

    www.countrywidepropertyauctions.co.uk

7. Martin & Pole

    Auctioneers specialising in the Berkshire area for over 160 years.

    www.martinpole.co.uk

8. Philip Arnold Auctioneers
   Formerly Brendons Auctioneers Ltd., successfully auctioning property nationwide with a focus on West London.
   www.philiparnoldauctions.co.uk

9. Savills
   Auctioning usually higher-end properties in central London and Nottingham.
   www.auctions.savills.co.uk

10. Shobrook & Co
    Cornwall-based auctioneer that conducts quarterly auctions featuring properties in need of renovation, are tenanted or part vacant investment properties, or properties of special interest.
    www.shobrook.co.uk

## *Buy-to-Let / Need-to-Know*

Investors in the buy-to-let market have a great responsibility beyond working towards their own profit-making. While many will take on a lettings agent or property manager to deal with the day-to-day tenancy issues, it is important to be aware of UK legislation surrounding property lets. According to BTL investment agency Select Property, the most important considerations include the following:

### Tenancy Protection Scheme

Tenancy deposit protection (TDP) schemes provide security for both tenants and landlords. The deposit paid by residents prior to moving into a property is placed into a protected government-backed account that neither the tenant nor the landlord has access to. When the tenancy contract ends, the landlord must agree how much of the deposit will be returned. The landlord may feel, for instance, justified in claiming part of the funds to pay for any property damage caused by the tenant. If both landlord and tenant agree on the amount to be returned, it will be paid back within 10 days of the tenancy's termination date. If the tenant disputes the amount, the tenant may contest it via a free dispute resolution service. Both parties present their case and a decision will be made.

## Health and Safety Requirements

Landlords who manage their own properties are fully responsible for ensuring their property meets UK health and safety legislation. Before letting can take place, several laws must be adhered to, from maintaining gas appliances to fitting the correct fire safety equipment to checking electrical sockets and appliances are safe to use.

## Property Maintenance

Landlords are required to maintain their properties to a good standard and fix any faults that occur. On occasion this may include being involved in emergency situations, for example if a burglary occurs or the heating breaks down.

## Rental Lease Agreements

When renting out your property, you create a contract between yourself and the resident. This contract grants the tenant with a leasehold estate, meaning that the tenant is given exclusive possession of the home for the period of the contract. The contract offers security to both landlord and tenant. UK legislation dictates that residents may renew their lease upon expiry on the same terms as the original lease. The landlord may reject the renewal request, but only in a few specific circumstances, such as wanting to live in the property themselves or they may want to redevelop it. The landlord must then give sufficient notice for the tenant to move out upon expiry of the original rental agreement.

\* \* \* \* \* \* \* \* \* \*

If you are based abroad, occurrences of property faults and tenant issues can be a real worry, therefore it makes sense to hire a local property manager to step in and deal with any problems that arise. The last thing you want is a frantic tenant who can't get the boiler to work calling you from thousands of miles away in the middle of the night – resulting in anxiety for both you and your tenant! Hiring a reputable and trustworthy manager is vital to protect your rental properties and to look after your tenants. Choose your management agency wisely; check they are a registered member of the UK Association of Lettings Agents (UKALA) which ensures their adherence to a Code of Practice, or the Association of Residential Lettings Agents.

## Glossary of Property Terms

**Auction** – The sale of a property to the highest bidder.

**Annual Percentage Rate** – The total cost of a loan, including all interest charges and arrangement fees, shown as a percentage rate and easily comparable with mortgage interest rates.

**Balance outstanding** – The amount of money or loan owed to the lender at a particular time.

**Bank** – A lending institution for mortgages.

**Building regulations** – The health and safety requirements that any new building or significant redevelopment must meet.

**Building society** – A mutual institution owned by its investors and borrowers that provides a range of savings and mortgage lending products; for example, the Nationwide Building Society.

**Buildings insurance** – Insurance against the cost of rebuilding a property from scratch following structural damage; for example, from fire, flood or storm.

**Capped rate mortgage** – A mortgage repayment scheme in which there is a fixed upper limit, or cap, to the interest payable, but where the standard variable interest rate applies when it is lower than the capped rate.

**Cash back mortgage** – A cash refund incentive offered by mortgage lenders to attract new borrowers, calculated as a small percentage of the mortgage advance.

**Commission** – The fee charged by estate agents, property consultants, or finders for finding the desired property for a buyer.

**Completion** – The point at which all financial transactions are complete and the purchaser becomes the legal owner of a property.

**Contents insurance** – Insurance against accidental damage or theft of all moveable contents, including furniture, appliances and soft furnishings.

**Conveyancer** – Legally trained individual who conducts the conveyance.

**Conveyancing** – The legal process involved in buying and selling property or land.

**Covenant** – An undertaking to do or not to do a certain course of action.

**Deposit** – The sum of money that the buyer puts down to secure the mortgage loan after the exchange of contracts; 10% of the purchase price, for example.

**Discharge or redeeming a mortgage** - Paying off a mortgage.

**Discounted rate mortgage** – A discount offered by mortgage lenders to new borrowers, reducing monthly mortgage costs often during the first two or three years of the loan period.

**Diversification** – The strategy of making several different investments (particularly stocks and shares) to spread out the risk of fluctuating values.

**Early Redemption** – The completion of mortgage repayments before the agreed upon term.

**Equity** – The difference between the value of a property and the amount of mortgage owed on it.

**Estate Agent** – An intermediary between a seller and a buyer who usually works on behalf of the seller.

**Exchange of contracts** – The time when the buying and selling of a property becomes legally binding.

**Fixed interest rate** – An interest rate that stays the same throughout the fixed period of the loan unlike the variable interest rate.

**Fixtures and fittings** – A term for all non-structural items included in the sale of a property.

**Flexible mortgage** – An arrangement enabling the mortgage borrower to increase and decrease payments as they wish (within certain limits).

**Freehold** – Absolute and indefinite ownership of a property.

**Gazundering** – A situation in which the buyer offers less than the agreed upon price just before exchange of contracts.

**Gazzumping** – A scenario in which the seller demands more money or accepts a higher offer, just before exchange of contracts.

**Ground rent** – The annual fee that a leaseholder pays to a freeholder.

**Home buyer's report** – A surveyor's report containing a valuation and details of the condition of the property.

**Indemnity premium** – An additional charge to cover the lender against higher risk to exposure when a mortgage is say, more than 75% of the property's value.

**Joint mortgage** – A mortgage shared jointly between two people with the agreement that if one dies the other automatically inherits the other share.

**Land Certificate** – A certificate from the Land Registry proving ownership of a property or land.

**Land Registry** – This is the government department that keeps a record of land ownership in the country.

**Mortgage** – A loan that is secured against a property.

**Mortgagee** – The mortgage lender, usually a bank or building society.

**Mortgagor** – The mortgage borrower.

**Multi-Agency** – The selection of two or more real estate agents to act on the seller's behalf, incurring a higher fee than if the sale is completed by sole agency.

**Negative Equity** – The shortfall between the value of a property and the outstanding sum owed on a mortgage.

**Offer** – The sum of money that the buyer offers to pay for a property.

**Planning permission** – This is the permission granted by the local planning authority (usually by the local council) for any new building, major extension, or change of use of a building.

**Preliminary enquiries** – Questions that the seller must answer before the exchange of contracts.

**Private Sale** – This refers to the sale of a property without the use of an estate agent as an intermediary.

**Redemption penalties** – Costs that may be incurred if the borrower repays the loan too early or switches to another lender.

**Re-mortgage** – The refinancing of a property by switching the mortgage from one lender to another with a new mortgage.

**Registered land** – Land for which ownership is registered at the land registry.

**Repayment mortgage** – A mortgage that accumulates monthly interest combined with payment towards the original sum borrowed.

**Retention** – The practice of holding back part of a mortgage loan until repairs to the property are satisfactorily completed.

**Sole agency** – The choice of a single estate agent to act on the seller's behalf, incurring a lower fee than a multi-agency sale.

**Solicitor** – A legal expert who handles all documentation for sale and purchase of a property.

**Stamp Duty** – A government tax on property purchases for those above a certain price determined by the government.

**Subject to Contract** – Term used in a property sale to indicate that an agreement is not yet legally binding.

**Survey** – Inspection of a property for any structural damage, dry rot, rising damp, etc., prior to the mortgage offer.

**Surveyor** – The person who carries out the survey on a property.

**Tenants** – People renting and living in a particular property.

**Tenants in common** – Property owners who have won unequal shares of a property and are free to dispose of their share in any way they wish.

**Title** – The legal ownership of a property or land.

**Title Deeds** – The legal document assigning ownership of a property or land.

**Transfer Deeds** – The Land Registry document that transfers legal ownership from seller to buyer.

**Under offer** – Term applied to a property for which the seller has provisionally accepted the buyer's offer.

**Valuation** – A surveyor's report required by the lender.

**Vendor** – The seller of a property or a plot of land.

# Useful Contacts

### The Bank of England

This is the central Bank of England and the model on which many of the world's modern central banks are based. They have many publications that offer insight into the state of the country's economy, which in turn could also prove invaluable to you as you plan to make your property investments or run new business in the United Kingdom.

Bank of England
Threadneedle Street, London, EC2R 8AH
Tel: +44 207 601 4878
Fax: +44 207 601 4771
E-mail: enquiries@bankofengland.co.uk
Website: www.bankofengland.co.uk

## Council of Mortgage Lenders (CML)

This is a not-for-profit organisation and the trade association for the mortgage lending industry, whose members account for around 95% of residential mortgage lending in the UK. These include banks, building societies and other mortgage lenders. If you need to obtain a mortgage from any of the members in their directory, their contact details are as follows:

Council of Mortgage Lenders
Bush House, North West Wing,
Aldwych, London WC2B 4PJ
Tel: 0845 373 6771
Fax: 0845 373 6778
Website: www.cml.org.uk

## GOV.UK

The first stop for all general enquiries regarding UK government services and information:

Website: www.gov.uk

## The Law Society of England & Wales

The independent professional body for solicitors. If you need a solicitor to do the conveyance of your property purchase, do a quick search via the website.

The Law Society of England & Wales
The Law Society's Hall, 113 Chancery Lane,
London WC2A 1PL
Tel: +44 207 242 1222   Fax: +44 207 831 0344
Website: www.thelawsociety.org.uk

## Timo Real Estate Solutions UK Ltd

If you are a domestic or foreign property investor looking for a reliable property finder, or a company that specialises in sourcing residential and commercial properties in London and throughout the whole of the United Kingdom, contact Timo Real Estate Solutions.

Website: www.timorealestatesolutions.co.uk

## UK Association of Letting Agents (UKALA)

The number one trade body representing letting and management agencies in the United Kingdom; also encompasses the National Association of Landlords.

UKALA
Skyline House, 200 Union St, London SE1 0LX
Tel: +44 20 7820 7900
Website: www.ukala.org.uk


## TOP UK HIGH STREET BANKS & BUILDING SOCIETIES

### Barclays PLC Headquarters
1 Churchill Pl, Canary Wharf, London E14 5HP
Tel: 0808 159 4947 or +44 20 7116 9000
Website: www.barclays.co.uk

### Halifax
Trinity Road, Halifax, West Yorkshire HX1 2RG
Tel: +44 843 557 3774   Website: www.halifax.co.uk

### HSBC
8 Canada Square, Canary Wharf, London E14 5HQ
Tel: +44 207 088 2077   Website: www.hsbc.co.uk

## Lloyds Banking Group
25 Gresham Street, London EC2V 7HN
Tel: 0345 300 0000 or +44 1733 347007
Website: www.lloydsbank.com

## Nationwide Building Society
Nationwide House, Pipers Way, Swindon SN38 1NW
Tel: 0800 30 20 10 (UK)
Website: www.nationwide.co.uk

## NatWest Bank
135 Bishopsgate, London EC2M 3UR
Tel: +44 844 453 0259
Website: www.nwolb.com

## Santander
10, The Mall, Manchester M30 0EA
Tel: 0800 068 6069
Website: www.santander.co.uk

## Yorkshire Building Society
Yorkshire House, Yorkshire Drive, Bradford, West Yorkshire BD5 8LJ
Website: www.ybs.co.uk

# Chapter 15
# Timo Real Estate Solutions

## *The One-Stop Shop*

As discussed throughout this book, it is essential to have a good team supporting you in your property investment ventures. My company, Timo Real Estate Solutions UK Ltd, is a one-stop shop of support and guidance, comprising a team of very experienced and customer-focussed individuals who offer a high-quality and bespoke personal service. We are therefore able to invest as much time and effort as necessary to ensure that we achieve the best possible results for you. Our clients are our number one priority!

We are here to help, whether you are buying your first home, selling your property, need a mortgage or you are an international property investor who wants to build a multi-million-pound property portfolio in London. Our company slogan is "Your needs come first", and so our primary goal is to identify your requirements and priorities at the outset. We will work with you to draw up an action plan and then deliver the necessary results for you in the shortest possible time!

We will go that extra mile for you to ensure that you are 100% satisfied with our product delivery and customer service. We are fully aware that a happy client will recommend and refer our services to friends and family if they have total confidence in us. Our aim is to build a long-term relationship with you based on honesty, integrity, transparency and professionalism.

**WHY CHOOSE US?**

- As a client, you will have unlimited access to exclusive property investment opportunities. We are well connected in the UK property industry and so we are able to source any type of property at lower or discounted prices (even at auctions), usually between 10-40% below the current market value. Our objective is to ensure that your money works harder for you by adding value to your property investment from day one.
- You will have one point of contact who shall give you exceptional, personal customer

service. Bearing in mind your personal circumstances and preferences, a dedicated member of our staff will be assigned to you to look after you and your interests. Our staff take great pride in building long-term relationships with all our clients now and in the future. You will also have direct access to the Managing Director, should you require a second opinion.

- You can rest assured that your property will be sold within an agreed timeframe if you instruct us to do so. Given our broad knowledge, vast experience and large client database of First-Time Buyers, Home Movers, Landlords and International Property Investors, we will ensure that the whole process of selling your property is as quick and smooth as possible!
- We are fully committed to providing excellent customer service, and guarantee you will have total peace of mind by taking away the hassle and stress of selling or buying a property. We will do whatever it takes to achieve a positive outcome for you. We aim to do so by keeping you constantly updated on any progress through communicating with all parties involved. Whenever necessary, we shall

contact solicitors, surveyors and banks on your behalf to keep the whole process on track.
- You will benefit from our thorough after-sales personal service. Once we have completed the transaction of selling your house or sourcing the right property for you and have obtained the most suitable mortgage for you, we will still be here for you in the long term. We appreciate, for instance, that your insurance protection may be up for renewal in the following years or your mortgage product may have to be reviewed in the future.

## OUR SERVICES

### SELLING

We sell properties on behalf of our clients who are normally home movers, landlords or property investors. As part of our service, you will receive an honest and realistic market appraisal of your property, we will arrange personal viewings for potential buyers, give you regular reports and updates without you having to chase us, and we will provide you with a complete professional and personal service from instruction to completion of the sale of your property.

## SOURCING

We source both residential and commercial properties at lower prices for all our clients who may be first-time buyers, landlords or property investors not only from within the UK but also from the following 20 carefully chosen countries:

*Middle East:*

Qatar, Oman, Kuwait, Bahrain,
United Arab Emirates, Saudi Arabia

*Far East:*

China, Indonesia, Japan, Philippines,
Thailand, Hong Kong, Singapore

*Africa:*

Kenya, South Africa, Rwanda,
Tanzania, Botswana, Ethiopia, Uganda

## LETTINGS AND PROPERTY MANAGEMENT

Letting a property can be a time consuming, stressful and aggravating experience. Our aim is to minimise or take away this stress and risk to you and your investment. We will therefore take the time to listen to you, understand your letting needs and then efficiently find the right tenant for your property. As part of our service to you, we will only recommend a tenant to you who has been checked through properly documented vetting or referencing. We shall give you an honest and realistic estimate of your property rental value in the current market, carry out inventory checks and give you a report every six months. We will also provide you with regular updates as well as take away from you all the hassle and stress of worrying about tenancy contracts, taxation and the deposit protection service to mention but a few.

## COMMERCIAL PROPERTY

You can rest assured that we will source the right commercial property or business for you as well as arranging the finance, if necessary. If your priority is to make profitable investments, especially in London, we shall find out what your needs are first, for example, purchasing and running a care home, hotel, restaurant, office buildings, retail shops, warehouses, factories or even blocks of apartments. Whether your budget is £200,000 or £1,000,000, we can source the right commercial property or business for you.

**FINANCIAL SERVICES**

We do understand that taking out a mortgage to buy a residential or commercial property is not only a challenging task, as there are countless lenders and mortgage products to choose from, but it is also likely to be your biggest financial commitment. It is therefore important that we listen clearly to your needs and requirements in order to be able to obtain the best mortgage deal for you. This is exactly what we do... sourcing what is best for you so that we can save you time and money in the long-term!

To this effect, it may be necessary for us (in some instances) to introduce you to some of our highly recommended and very experienced Mortgage / Financial Planning Consultants or Wealth Managers who will take care of everything for you. We will ensure that you get a full mortgage/financial, wealth creation and protection review so that you are offered the best products, not only to buy that new dream home or property investment but also to protect it, should the unexpected happen.

Our promise to you:

- You will get reliable and prompt customer service from us as our sole objective is to make you our loyal customer for life.
- You will appreciate the value of your property from day one, for instance, you shall have equity in your investment coupled with excellent after-sales service.
- You will be given impartial and honest advice throughout the whole process of selling or buying a property with us.
- You will be dealing with us directly on a personal level. You are not simply another number to us but an individual for whom we will work tirelessly, in order to win your trust and business.
- As a client who wants timely positive results, you shall be pleased to know that we are not only so passionate about what we do and all types of properties but we are also target driven and very focussed on delivering the best results for you in the shortest time possible!

\* \* \* \* \* \* \* \* \*

As we arrive at the end of this book, the message I want to convey to you is this: there is no time like the present to pursue the success you desire. I have demonstrated a number of ways you can achieve wealth through diverse opportunities in the UK real estate market. If an immigrant from Uganda can do it, so can you!

No matter where you are in the world, Timo Real Estate Solutions can help make that journey to property investment success as smooth as possible.

## Acknowledgements

I am eternally grateful to the following people, those who have played a significant role in the development of this book and others who have had a major positive impact on my life.

Nichola Tyrrell, my new great friend whose input and contribution to this book has been so invaluable and will always be appreciated... Thank you so, so much for the exemplary job of editing this book very well.

Stephanie Hale – your expertise never ceases to amaze me, week in week out.

Charmaine Tesaga – What are great friends for? You have given me so much moral support that has not only kept me sane but has also given me the positive energy to persevere. You're simply one in a million!

Buddy Roberts, my "Top Bro", and the little Princesses, Erica & Libby. Carol Rhona Mukasa Kayemba, "My Rock", and great buddy Michael Mukasa. Angela Walakira, Clare Turner-Marshall, Tanya Daye "The Cool Virtual Entrepreneur",

Christopher Mulinde (My Great Buddy), Rosario Lee (My Great Inspirational Guru), the late Charles Karegyesa, William Mpalanyi, Charles Mukasa, Tracey Mackenzie – What shall I ever do without you?

Elizabeth Kibalama, "my Guardian Angel", whom I will always be very grateful indeed to, for standing by me during those difficult times... Thank you, Thank you, Thank you!

Robert Kasirye Musoke – Thank you so much for everything Sir, Ben Miller for always believing in me and for giving me lots of hope for the future,

Gobnait Cronin, Mr D Hirani, Mr Arvind Kohli, Bishop Trevor Mwamba. Lisa Jeffs – a special lady in more ways than one.

Andy Kupoloyi, Anil Hirani, Vince Thomas, Joy Lubega, you are such a true and great friend... Do you remember that tricky trip in Brixton?

Tuvude wala, right? I really treasure our chats too!!! Dorian and my cute nephew, Joel. Cathy and Andrew Zzimbe, Ezra and Resty Lugoloobi with my nieces, Vanessa, Karen, Ruth and Veronica. Peter, Dorah and the lovely little ones. Ruth and my nephew, Favour. Lisa Cousins... What can I say? Top Lady you are!

Auntie Alice, Mr Richard and Mrs Robinah Golola as well as Jackie, Solome, Jessica and the little Prince. Mr Godfrey and Mrs M Kavuma, Mr Duncan and Mrs Miriam Neville, Mr V & Mrs J Mukiibi coupled with Jan Mukiibi (Miss Uganda UK 2017), Mr Ali Mutebi and Ms Jessica Walusimbi as well as Zani, Quays and Nassuna. Mrs Barbara Vuvu, Sarah Nakaddu, Samantha Nattabi, Lydia Kajubi, John Mbuga, David Kamuzze, Ronald Kitanda, All Agaffa e Uganda Group Members, Tracey and Mwami Sendi, Betsy and Mr Ali and family, Annette and Albert Ntege, Mr Ben Miller – "The Tele-Marketing Guru", the late Babba "Robert Gita" and the late Babba Margaret. Sarah Nakaddu, Philip Wabulya, Martin Rubagumya, Hopes Kikonyogo, All UK Buddo crew and the entire Abageeti Group Members.

The late Jajja Kasirye – I am still proud to be your favourite grandchild.

My Dad and my Dear Late Mum, "Miima", I miss you lots!

Olivia G S Muwanguzi ... Thank you SO, so much for everything Madam!!!

Kirsty Marietta Muwanguzi . . . You are the reason I have had countless, sleepless nights thinking about your future. I love you so much, to the moon and back!

www.timoseks.com

www.ingramcontent.com/pod-product-compliance
Lightning Source LLC
Chambersburg PA
CBHW020642220526
45464CB00001B/260